# Wrong
## Place

# Right *at the*
## Time

Quantity discounts are available on bulk orders.
Contact info@TAGPublishers.com for more information.

TAG Publishing, LLC
2618 S. Lipscomb
Amarillo, TX 79109
www.TAGPublishers.com
Office (806) 373-0114
Fax (806) 373-4004
info@TAGPublishers.com

ISBN: 978-1-934606-39-1

First Edition

Cover Design by Jerrod McReynolds

# Wrong Place
## at the
# Right
## Time

*How a Dose of Humility Led to Victory*

*Dawn Taylor Wells*

*I dedicate this book to my two sisters, Tanya and Terri. After fighting many battles, I am so thankful that we found our strength through a loving God Who never leaves us nor forsakes us. A three strand cord is difficult to break. Always remember, there's a place for us. I love you both very much.*

*I also dedicate this book to all the men, women and children who patiently sit through hours of dialysis to live. Your strength, courage and faith is remarkable and I commend you for never giving up.*

They overcame him by the blood of the Lamb and by the word of their testimony; they did not love their lives so much as to shrink from death.

Revelation 12: 11

# Acknowledgments

First and foremost, I thank Jesus Christ, my Lord and Savior. I am nothing without Him. Because of His never-ending love and redemption, I have purpose and meaning in my life.

I thank my husband, Gary, for his unconditional love and support throughout the process of writing this book. His encouragement and belief in me sustained my efforts when doubt and insecurity crept in. This book would have never made it to print had it not been for Gary's love. Six years of writing required five years of healing. Gary, I love you with all of my heart and thank you for being my earthly redeemer; my gift from God.

A special thank you to Dee Burks with TAG Publishing who has worked many hours with me on this project and helped make this a book worth reading. Dee, your belief in me and this book catapulted me to want to share it with everyone. Your hours of editing expertise helped make this book interesting and useful, rather than my boring memoir. Thank you from the bottom of my heart.

A heartfelt thank you goes to the Writing Life Group I attended for several months. Your constructive criticism and enormous encouragement helped me get started. A special thank you to Kathy Stevens for answering my many questions about publishing and for hosting our Life Group in her lovely home. To our fearless leader, Glenda Lowery, thank you for your knowledge, love and genuine concern for all of us as writers and encouraging us to write, write, write!

To all my dear friends and family who have cheered me on to finish this book and given me their continued support and encouragement. Thank you for believing in me!

# Contents

# Introduction

One of my favorite television shows is about a complete fashion transformation. I'm not talking about a 'makeover.' No, this is truly a transformation. They take requests from people all around the country whose loved one is in dire need of a major fashion overhaul. The winner flies to New York City with their old clothes in tow, and then agrees they'll throw away anything that does not enable them to move forward from a fashion stand point. For most, it's their entire wardrobe. For a person who obviously doesn't have much fashion sense, (hence their nomination) getting everything in their wardrobe thrown out could be quite frightening. I mean, think about it . . . you have to start all over from scratch! You have to build a wardrobe in a week, with $5000 and all new fashion rules, most of which are foreign. I love watching this show, and I can empathize with the nominee's distress in starting over and deciding on some new 'style' that would be fitting for them and their future.

To me, this show is all about letting go of the past. The clothing represents all those characteristics that inhibit a person from moving forward. I don't know how many times I've hung on to a pair of jeans that I skip over every day I get dressed, and won't get rid of. Why? I don't like to wear them, so why don't I toss them and make room for a new pair I love? That is how it is with emotional baggage, too. Why don't we get rid of that ratty suitcase full of old behaviors and thoughts? Doesn't it make sense to replace them with more productive behaviors that actually do work for our life now?

Throughout the process of the fashion transformation, most people begrudgingly give up their favorite sweat shirts, or clogs or whatever it is they feel the need to hang onto for dear life. They are usually afraid to take on a new style that they have never envisioned, and the fear of the unknown paralyzes them. I suspect one of the reasons I love that show is because I relate my life to a total transformation as well. For years, I wandered through my life wearing numerous worn-out thoughts, attitudes and carrying my own heavy emotional baggage that served no productive or healthy purpose whatsoever. I clung to the sadness, loneliness and grief that I encountered as a young child. I clothed myself in bad habits like an old polyester pant suit. Those habits didn't flatter me or help me move forward any better than that pant suit. My coping skills were similar to four-inch stilettos: great in appearance, but not practical or comfortable.

I stumbled into surrendering my life to new and better guidelines while wearing those four inch stilettos one night at a bar. God attempted on numerous occasions to get my attention, but I refused to listen. No, I imagined how fabulous I appeared with those heels, not realizing everyone else saw the truth—that I was miserable. He waited for me a very long time to get to that specific place, and I finally arrived, stumbling down drunk and humiliated beyond belief. I had all my negative thoughts and attitudes, useless coping skills, shame, guilt and condemnation in tow – it was quite a sight.

I also had a lot of loneliness and fear packed in that suitcase I'd carried around for years like a ratty, but comfortable blanket. I was a complete mess and I needed a big God to transform me.

He was certainly up for the task.

Not only did He clean me up and give me a new emotional wardrobe and outlook, He gave me a new heart. You see, it was my heart that was so terribly bruised and beaten from the events and circumstances I had experienced. I carried all that pain with me and along the way, I learned some destructive behaviors to contend with it. None of those behaviors worked to alleviate the pain permanently and I was on an endless cycle of self destruction. I needed a Savior and He was ready and willing to take me on.

Even though He dragged me out of the mud and muck of what I'd made of my life, it took me a long time to get to a place of understanding not only of myself, but of the grace I'd been offered. The interesting thing is that if someone told me back then that it was even possible for me to live in freedom and with peace of mind, I would have laughed – and ordered another round. I did not believe for one second that the mess I'd created could ever lead to something good. I believed I was bad; I did bad things and my punishment was always close at hand. I believed the lies the enemy so cunningly handed me and didn't think twice about it.

I don't live that way today. Needless to say, I didn't do it alone. None of us do. I had help along my journey from people who chose to see the possibilities for me even when I was convinced they didn't exist. My story of redemption started with that bad night, a hefty dose of humiliation and a really hard lesson in life. It was a night I will never forget, but it was also the first step to a beautiful and life altering transformation. I never dreamed I'd thank God for that night, but today, I do, over and over.

You may be thinking it's just not possible for you to live a life of freedom and peace, but I'm here to tell you that you are wrong, just as I was. Oh, make no mistake; I understand where you are at right now and can relate to the very same emotions; the disappointment, the reluctance to get your hopes up, and the guilt from all those times you tried to change before and failed. Believe me, I feel your pain as strongly as I felt my own back then. But there is hope and I wrote this book for you.

I want to take you on a journey of how God's relentless pursuit and all-consuming love transformed my life and can transform yours as well. God's love and grace is undeniable and ever-present and I thank Him every day for the new life He gave me. Never would I have imagined what God had in store once I surrendered everything to Him.

I'm not going to lie to you; surrendering my life to Jesus has not always been easy. I was never the 'surrender' kind of gal. I controlled my life, or so I thought, no matter how miserable that life may have been. The changes I chose to make to receive

His wonderful blessings came at a high price, and I still endure adversity along the path, but the rewards of walking with Jesus far outweigh the trials. I was one of those lukewarm, part-time believers for many years and it wasn't until I could go no further in the state I was in that I finally gave it all to Jesus. That one decision transformed not only who I was, but who I could be.

My life may be similar to yours, or quite different, but I suspect if you're reading this book, we desire the same result: to live an abundant life of joy free from past hurts and heartaches and emotional baggage incurred over time. Not only did God heal my wounds, end my pain and fill my heart with joy, I also gained an all-in, loving relationship with Jesus Christ. The knowledge that I will spend eternity in Heaven with Him gives me a peace that I carry with me every day. I had no idea at the time, but peace was a foreign concept in my daily life. I existed in chaos, fear, stress and panic most of the time. The difference now is vast and it not only saved my soul, but probably spared me dozens of wrinkles as well.

No matter where you've been or what you've done, you can have a life of freedom, peace, joy and purpose, too. It awaits you, my friend, it does for everyone. The change for me didn't happen all at once. I had some good days and some bad days and some painful days, too. It has been an ongoing process with lots of growth along the way. None of us are ever perfect or will ever 'arrive' fully in this life and we aren't intended to; we are here to learn and grow into the likeness of Jesus. The wonderful discovery I've made is that you cannot hide a changed heart. It's simply impossible. A heart that has healed and awoken to the glory and power within is evident to all those who see it.

My wish for you is that there is something in these words that gives you a new hope—a hope that transcends all your fears of what living a different way might mean for you. I'd wanted to change for years, but the fear of the unknown kept me shackled. It took me being in the wrong place at the right time for God to get my attention. My stubbornness all those years came to a head that one fateful night, and my life has never been the same. That particular night, I tripped over myself and fell right into the arms of God.

# Chapter One

## *A Night to Remember*

*Thank goodness for Happy Hour.* I arrived at the martini bar one chilly Friday night in February 2003 after leaving work. I was never that fond of martinis, but even that sounded good to me right about then. I loved the social camaraderie at any given bar around the Happy Hour time of day. Most patrons were there to relax with the subtle effects of the alcohol they consumed over the next few hours and shake off the day's worries.

I enjoyed Happy Hour because it gave me the freedom to feel good for a short time and to numb my pain from a lifetime of guilt, shame, condemnation and abandonment. I longed for the moment when the alcohol ran through my veins and all that pain subsided for a few hours. Undoubtedly, I was a much different person underneath the persona of the happy-go-lucky social butterfly I projected. For as long as I could remember, insecurities, loneliness and a sense of inadequacy plagued me to the marrow of my bones. The weight of my mistakes over the past twenty years of life and heart break from people I loved never lifted long enough for me to envision being a happy, successful person someday.

*For now, I think I'll have another drink.*

I left that bar and headed home after several cocktails. I'd been home for only a short time when a friend called and asked if I'd go out with her to another bar.

"I'm already in for the night," I replied. *Safe and sound, thank goodness.*

After minimal persuasion, I agreed to go out with her, but only if she drove. I at least had the sense to know I shouldn't drive in my condition. My friend picked me up and we traveled to a local bar nearby, which happened to be an establishment my ex-husband was known to frequent.

I resisted. "No! I'm not going in there! What if he's inside?"

We drove through the parking lot and once I realized his vehicle wasn't there, we decided it was safe to go inside.

I do recall that for a Friday night, the place seemed quiet and barren. I wondered if some event was going on that took the regulars away. We ambled up to the bar and plopped ourselves down on a bar stool and ordered our first of many cocktails. I felt quite smug as I sat there enjoying this old, familiar hangout. It had been almost a year since the last time I was there. The very thought of me being there seemed rebellious and risky. This was a place I'd spent many nights sitting on top of a barstool during my marriage. If only walls could talk.

After several drinks, to my astonishment, my ex-husband's girlfriend walked in.

Oh, this is going to be good! I thought. With my small frame and build, I'm no contender for a physical fight, but I could verbally spar with the best of them. I was ready.

My blood was full of alcohol now and I had enough pride rolling through my veins that I felt quite confident to address my adversary. She and her friend, sat down on the bar stool right next to me.

*Really? You had to sit right here, when there's five other chairs to sit on?*

My heart pumped harder and faster and I knew a confrontation was imminent. The provocation began as I loudly asked my friend, "Did she have to sit right next to me when there are five other bar stools to sit on?"

My friend smirked and gave me that look that implied, *Dawn, calm down. Don't start an argument.*

As was my intent, my adversary took the bait, and we were soon trading insults and verbal jabs with the gusto of prize fighters. Oh, it got ugly fast. My vain insecurities rose to the surface within seconds. Caustic remarks flew from my mouth and were hurtful, intentional and foolish. I didn't care. This confrontation was long overdue and I was determined to speak my intoxicated mind. Out of my mouth flew another cutting remark and within seconds, she struck out. I pulled my face to one side as her fist swept across my neck.

*Did she just take a swing at me?* I could not believe it. I was no match for her in a real battle; she could have taken me down in a second.

The bartender asked her to leave since she took the first, and thankfully, only swing. She was none too happy to leave the familiar establishment. After all, this was her and my ex's hangout now, not mine. While I felt a little deserving of the punch, I was thankful she was the one asked to leave. One more attempted swing from her could have easily knocked me off my bar stool.

As the night wore on, the story manifested itself into a much more dramatic event than I ever imagined. In some ways, I loved the drama. It took my mind off of my pain for a moment and added some excitement to my lackluster life. As a child, I became familiar with drama and chaos, so in some sick way, it was comforting. My friend and I had plenty to gossip about now and with anyone who would listen. We finished up a few more drinks and continued down the street to another bar. There, we met a few friends and shared our juicy bit of drama with them. Oh, how a morsel of gossip draws people close and we all knew that this was some great gossip. I continued to intoxicate myself that night with reckless abandon. Although I'd just been in a near altercation with my ex-husband's girlfriend, you would have thought by my behavior I'd just run a marathon – and won. With adrenaline pumping, I was gleaming with excitement to tell the story for the next several hours to anyone and everyone who would listen.

My friend and I were obviously too drunk to drive ourselves home, so a couple of guys we knew gave us a ride back to my house. Knowing I had a bottle of champagne in the refrigerator, I invited everyone in to celebrate the night's drama. The four of us continued to drink until every last drop of champagne was drained. In the wee hours of the morning, after discussing the night's events to exhaustion, we fell asleep. That was one of the longest nights of my life. Thank goodness it finally ended.

When consciousness knocked on my door the next morning, I thought it was a sledgehammer banging on my head. I'd never experienced a headache like that in all my years of drinking— and there had been many. I couldn't swallow six aspirin quickly enough to stop the thundering in my skull. My mouth was as dry as the Sahara desert in July. I could hardly talk.

*Water. I need water.*

In a tiny corner of my mind, the thought of what happened the night before tried to peek out but I shoved it down. I didn't want to think about it yet. Physically, I needed relief before I could mentally go through the humiliating events of last night and consider the possible ramifications. My body ached so badly, even the flu would have seemed like a sweet reprieve.

My friend finally awoke with a similar feeling in her aching body, but I don't think to the degree I suffered. The first words out of my mouth were something like, "I cannot believe what happened last night."

The events didn't affect her in the same manner as they had me. I was the subject of the controversial night, she was merely a bystander. I continued to proclaim how horribly I acted. I suppose that in some desperate way, I needed someone to forgive my actions. My friend didn't think I acted that badly at all.

*What? Were you even there last night? I am so ashamed of myself; I can't bear to see my reflection in the mirror!*

The emotional hangover had reared its ugly head and I was in a spiral of expanding shame and guilt. My friend didn't have an emotional hangover, so she couldn't understand why I was so hard on myself. Utterly disgusted and humiliated is how I can best describe my feelings. However, I was determined not to beat myself up, so I convinced myself that my friend was right; I hadn't acted so horribly. I mean, my friend was there, too, and she saw everything. Maybe I wasn't as despicable as I thought I was.

Still, I needed more confirmation, so we called a couple more allies to get their input. They immediately came over to hear about the exciting drama from the night before. After hearing all the facts, they didn't think I was out of line either.

*Oh, thank goodness, more confirmation. Finally, I can stop being so hard on myself.*

Three people had affirmed that how I behaved the night before was fine and totally appropriate for the given situation. To hear their words brought only temporary relief from my emotional hangover because deep down, I knew better. The gnawing humiliation continued to burn inside me.

After my friends left, I sat on my couch, deep in thought. I rehearsed the events of the night over and over in my mind – at least the ones I could remember for certain. I tried to rationalize my behavior and justify my actions to ease the ghastly guilt that continued to pound my soul. I couldn't get away from it. I couldn't wash it off in the shower. I couldn't cover it with makeup. I couldn't shake it from my thoughts.

*What kind of person acts like that and what exactly was I trying to prove? Who had I become?* That tormenting thought continued to billow in my mind. No matter what I did to change that thought, it kept coming back to haunt me. *Who have you become, Dawn?*

As I knew all too well, with guilt came the shame and soon thereafter, the condemnation. I'd spent years toting those three heavy bags around with me and even small events would send them crashing into my self-worth – and this was no small event, it was a whopper. I could not escape what had transpired the night before and by this time the news had traveled to numerous people. Even though I lived in a city of a couple hundred thousand, it was still a lot like a small town and everyone knows everyone. I imagined all the scandalous debate going on at my expense.

*Oh, goodness, what have I done?* At that moment, I was too ashamed to address or even think about God. In fact it was one of the times in my life I almost hoped God didn't know I existed, because if He did, I was certainly a huge disappointment and failure in His eyes. *How will I ever live through this?*

That day, Saturday, went on forever. Not only did my body ache worse than it ever had from a night of drinking, my mind was in agony and my heart was heavy with shame. The clock ticked the seconds off in slow motion. Usually, I would go out again and drink to relieve some of the pain, but the thought of alcohol passing my lips made my stomach churn.

I finally decided I needed some kind of distraction and should get out of the house, so I met my girlfriends at a restaurant lounge. My friends were completely unaware, but I brought my trusty three bags of emotional luggage right along with me - guilt, shame and condemnation. My load seemed heavier by the minute and my body was not up to carrying all that around on that particular day. However, I assumed I never had a choice and that guilt, shame and condemnation went everywhere I went, *faithfully*. My friends suggested I order a drink, that maybe it would make me feel better. The thought of that seemed inconceivable. I ordered a diet soda instead thinking it would at least give me some immediate comfort.

*Nope. Not a chance.* I could hardly stand my own company by this point and decided to go on home. As friends do, they encouraged me that I would feel better tomorrow and not to worry about it. More than anything, I wanted tomorrow to get here and be done with it. I wanted to escape today's pain. My thoughts became compulsive and I could not get away from them as humiliation settled in like a dense fog.

It was early evening and I put on my pajamas. I was in for the night and certainly did not want company. However, the company I could not get away from or avoid was me. Humiliation and shame grew inside me like a tumor. Every few minutes, some memory of the previous night flashed through my mind and I shook my head in disbelief. It was no longer an amusing bit of juicy drama, this was real. The events from the night before unlocked Pandora's box and memories of my past came rising to the surface of my mind. In one night, the heavily locked chest that successfully held years of self-loathing, fear, loneliness and wretchedness was thrust open to display my innermost self.

*How on earth did I arrive at this destination in my journey? Was this it for me? Would I continue to live a life full of guilt, shame and condemnation? Would this humiliation ever leave? Would I ever belong to someone again? Could God possibly help a wretch like me?*

As Shorty, my beloved Dachshund and I lay in bed that night, I was closely accompanied by those three loyal followers: guilt, shame and condemnation. I wondered how on Earth I became this person. *What lead me to this dreadful destination?* The questions were endless, and I had no answers. In the clutches of my followers, I finally fell into a restless sleep.

# Chapter Two

## *Happiness Is An Inside Job*

This was not how I thought life would turn out. In all my wildest dreams, I never imagined I'd find myself, at the age of thirty-eight, divorced, miserable, lonely, humiliated and completely disillusioned with my life. Where did it all go wrong? There was such a clash of expectations. Early on, I dreamed that by the age of twenty-five, I would be happily married to a wonderful man, and I would be his perfect wife. That dream emerged from a fantasy somewhere within the deep recess of my heart as it was something I'd never experienced. Perhaps the fantasy came from watching chick flicks or soap operas or even The Brady Bunch. Living in denial and focusing on unrealistic dreams was my way to escape the reality of a life of disappointment. We all dream, even if those dreams are unrealistic.

When I finally came to the end of my own rope, I knew this was not what I'd always hoped and dreamed for. Although, for as long as I could remember, I'd harbored a sense of unworthiness, insignificance and, at times, I even felt unlovable. I thought there was something terribly wrong with me. Yet that never changed the dream I carried inside—that one day I'd magically live a happily ever after kind of life.

However, here I was, divorced, in debt to the tune of $25,000, a humiliated, emotional wreck and faced with the realization that I was going to have to start all over again. The sad thing was I couldn't blame anyone but myself, no matter how much I wanted to blame my failures on my childhood, my parents' divorce and their dysfunction, or even my ex-husband. As a child, I internalized my feelings and harbored such distress that I had no idea how to feel better. There wasn't a day that went by that I didn't consider what a failure I was at something. I desperately hid my inner feelings because it was so important that people liked and approved of me. I put on a happy face almost every day, yet my soul was slowly and painfully dying.

I felt like a fake and a phony, but I wasn't about to let my façade slip for one second. Pride is a thief of happiness and contentment but I clung to mine like a life preserver. Unfortunately, it left a wake of destruction behind me as wide as the Grand Canyon. The problem is that pride can be quite difficult for a person to recognize. Believing I was right and being able to prove it was sometimes the most important thing to me in a relationship. I wanted to ensure I won every battle, even if it cost me the war. Yet, I didn't recognize that as pride. Feeling superior gave me the false sense of security and significance. Even when I saw how damaging this behavior was, I still continued to act that way because underneath, I felt inadequate and unimportant. I was more determined to be right than happy. I was willfully ignorant to the fact that pride was an invisible thief of my joy and happiness and, though I was convinced that it let people see me in a positive way, the truth was it actually put my insecurities on display for all to view.

Pride comes in many different forms and depending on the motive; it takes on varying facets for a person, some positive and some negative. Taking pride in one's work is a positive form when it motivates you to do your job well. But my pridefulness was of a different nature because it came from a motive of perfectionism. I deeply desired for people to believe I had it all together and so I played the part as best I could. In reality, I had no self-confidence, so I clung to the approval of others and their flattery. I was plagued with a gnawing fear that if people really saw who I was, it would destroy any positive opinion anyone ever had of me.

That Saturday, after making a fool of myself the night before, I knew the charade I was living had to end. I was exhausted and could no longer keep the act up. For many years, I'd pointed my finger at others and blamed them for my unhappiness, taking no responsibility for my own joy and fulfillment. The bottom line was this: *no one was responsible for my happiness except me.* I can't make someone happy and they can't make me happy. However, I could, and had, made myself incredibly miserable.

I'm not sure I'd ever really experienced true happiness in my life; in fact, I had no idea what it actually looked like. I knew that if I was ever to attain it, I had to find out what happiness meant for me. Along my journey, I discovered that happiness springs forth from a heart capable of housing contentment. But if a heart is burdened with wounds and unmet needs, it certainly cannot hold happiness in it at the same time. I had no idea at the time but I had to unload all the clutter of previous wounds, guilt, shame and negative events before happiness would be able to even find a room in my heart.

Happiness is such a subjective, sometimes elusive phenomenon. Webster's Dictionary defines happiness as 'a state of wellbeing and contentment.' Yet, what is considered well or content to one person could be dissatisfying to another. Now add to that idea that happiness shifts, moves and changes as our lives travel along. What I thought brought me happiness in my twenties and thirties I now considered to be stupid and self-destructive.

Throughout my life, many changes occurred, many that I had no control over and assumed I had to live with. Going through so many difficult and unwanted changes caused happiness to elude me - or so I thought. Because of the huge fear of anyone's disapproval, I allowed everyone else to dictate my life and my choices. I have since learned that happiness is a choice; but that is helpful *only* if you know it's a choice. During this time in my life when I was struggling, I thought you went out and found happiness like some kind of Easter egg hunt. What I have since discovered is that you make the decision to be happy. It doesn't just happen to you. You have to know how to choose it.

For those of you who feel happiness has eluded you all of your life, you're on common ground with how I felt. It's impossible to choose happiness if you're unaware it is, in fact, a choice. Most of my life, I believed my bouts of happiness were limited to only a quick burst of fake euphoria that lost its spark almost as quickly as it lit up in my heart. These bursts of euphoria depended on external circumstances, never internal. For example, if a man complimented me, for a brief moment I was happy that I actually appealed to someone. I felt noticed and significant at that moment in time, but almost as soon as his last complimentary word was spoken, the brief happiness escaped me once again. This created a behavior where I sought to impress another person to illicit some positive reaction or compliment from them, even if it was only temporary. As I consistently placed unrealistic expectations on my relationships and myself, I inevitably walked away disappointed. No matter how hard I tried, I could not seem to have a fulfilling relationship, or at least, my fantasy of a fulfilling relationship.

I had no idea what healthy boundaries were in a relationship – in fact I had no idea what boundaries even meant. I had some strange notion that in a relationship you had to be all and give all to the other person. I didn't know there could be definitions of where I stopped and the other person began. For this reason, I allowed people into my life who were also unfamiliar with boundaries in a relationship. Having little respect for myself, I never required it from others. Unhealthy people tend to attract unhealthy people.

Healthy people tend to attract healthy people. Friendships, family and intimate relationships are all affected by the emotional 'maturity and health of each person. That seems like such a simplistic and obvious observation, but yet, it is something that I was clueless about for decades. A vicious cycle ensued during my search for happiness as I continued to attract people who were as unsuccessful in relationships as I was. So in every attempt, I came up empty handed. Cheap external thrills that lasted momentarily left me emptier than before their surge of excitement. Not only did I not achieve happiness, I was even more disappointed in myself for all the failed relationships I had under my belt. Pride is so deceitful because it keeps us from ever honestly looking at what part we might have in the problem. Pride always tells us, "If they would just change, we might have a great relationship."

When someone experiences happiness only from outside sources, they are in fact, only experiencing an illusion of happiness. Happiness will remain at the mercy of the external source continually disappointing the one who so desires it. This is a depressing way to live. I too, believed happiness was from somewhere out there.

Convinced that being married, being single, making more money, driving a new car, having a better job, living in a different city, being prettier, smarter, taller, thinner, having blonde hair, longer hair or shorter hair, (the list goes on forever) certainly *that* would make me happy. To my dismay, none of the above brought true, lasting happiness. What I didn't realize as I tried to manipulate my external world, was that until I looked into my heart to see what had taken up residence, happiness would always be out of my reach no matter how many things I tried.

As I searched for happiness, the only thing I was consistent with was my inconsistencies. One day I followed God, the next day I ran from Him. I was inconsistent in my relationships and could not enjoy the present. I was plagued with guilt and regrets of the past and sometimes paralyzing fear and dread of the future. I had no peace in my life, but desperately desired it. I knew I couldn't keep up the pace forever and that somewhere something had to give. Proverbs 13:12 states, "hope deferred makes the heart sick, but a longing fulfilled is a tree of life." To me that said by pushing down and squashing any sense of hope for myself, I was making my own heart sick and that is exactly how I felt—*sick*.

Happiness was not a state of mind I recall either of my parents exhibiting in their own relationship. As a child, I never learned happiness was an internal state of well-being. I had no concept of what 'well-being' even meant. My internal state had always been marred with anxiety and fear. Nothing inside me ever felt well or content.

It took a large dose of humility for me to set aside my pride and take a good, hard look at my life. My life was a mess because *I* messed it up. There was no denying that fact. I'd taken the long road around the same mountain for many years and kept arriving at the same destination: misery. I sadly realized the common denominator in all my troubles was ME.

After unsuccessfully attempting to change everything on the outside, and present myself as perfect as I could, I reluctantly realized that happiness was an inside job. There was nothing I could change in the past and I had no control over the future. It was time to stop living the charade. Yet, I had no idea how to live another way. I continued to struggle with my behavior, but knew I wanted something different. I had no concept of what normal looked like; nonetheless, I deeply desired a calm, chaos-free life. I needed a new Dawn in every way.

I learned happiness is not a destination or a place one finally arrives. It's an intricate journey and along the way are numerous twists and turns. I had so much to learn and unlearn about the source of my own happiness. I now define happiness as: living at peace and being content with my authentic self. It truly is an internal state of well-being and contentment.

On my journey to find happiness, I uncovered beliefs about my past and understood that what I thought of as normal all those years was actually quite abnormal. Growing up in a dysfunctional, alcoholic home was a breeding ground for chaos and a classroom for the unhealthiest possible behaviors. I love my parents tremendously and know they did the best they could with what they had, but they did not have a healthy relationship and their dysfunction laid an extremely weak foundation for me. I watched their relationship disintegrate and that became my 'normal' for many years.

As a young girl, I learned that what went on around me, the external, was what controlled happiness, or caused pain. If I could control my surroundings, I could control my happiness. What a lie. This was engrained in who I was and it took many long, painful years to unlearn that one false belief.

# Chapter Three

## A Broken Little Girl

As far back as I can remember, I lived in fear—the kind of fear that paralyzes a person. I was the youngest of three daughters to a full-blood Lebanese father and a full-blood feminist mother. (I still don't know exactly how they got together.) By the time I reached the age of seven, I'd seen and heard hideous arguments between my parents. Both my parents were passionate, strong-willed people, determined to have things their way. At that young age, I had no idea that my parents' behavior was wrong or abnormal. It was all I'd seen and all I knew. When they argued, a knot tied itself up in my stomach and anxiety and nervousness was the inevitable result. What I didn't know was the incredible impact this would have on me and how it would dictate the next three decades of my life.

Late one night, I remember Dad and Mom arguing rather loudly. That was not unusual since they argued most of the time. This particular night, their words seemed louder and angrier than ever before and a knot tightened in my stomach as I listened to them yell. They called each other terrible names, screamed obscenities to each other and seemed more upset than I'd ever heard. I could barely stand the agony of listening to them fight. My sister, Terri, and I shared a bedroom and our window faced the front of the house. Terri couldn't sleep through the yelling either and she tried to comfort me by hugging me and telling me it was going to be okay. As the argument escalated, anxiety rose up inside me and she was unable to console me. I feared Dad was going to hit Mom.

The front door opened and slammed shut as Dad yelled to Mom, "Get out!" I looked out my bedroom window and saw Mom stumbling to her car. She got in and slammed the door shut so hard I jumped. I was afraid for her since she seemed so angry when she left; I feared she'd crash her car. I also felt sorry for her and wanted her to come back. I couldn't understand why Dad kicked her out. What I didn't realize was that he was drawing a line with Mom to protect us. She chose alcohol to deal with her pain. I'm sure my dad was not the easiest person to be married to either. But as a seven year old, I didn't understand all the nuances of their relationship.

When Dad yelled, it could all but sear a hole right through me. Unfortunately, Dad yelled quite often. That particular night's argument led to Mom and Dad's second and final divorce. I was devastated and ashamed of their break-up. There are so many details of parental arguments a child should never know about, hear about, or witness. Yet, my parents' lack of boundaries caused me to hear and see more than I ever could process as a seven year old.

I felt like a misfit with my peers because at the time, none of their parents were divorced. I felt "less-than" by having divorced parents. I hated the way I felt because there was nothing I could do to make my parents get back together (not that I didn't try.) It was during this time of my life that a door opened and shame and guilt slithered in. I was a shy child by nature, and the anxiousness and fearfulness that welled up inside me from all the arguments between my parents and their subsequent divorces caused me to internalize a sense of failure. Somehow, I thought I was the reason Mom left us. At seven years old, I couldn't differentiate their unhealthy behavior from my pain. Mom was an alcoholic. She was depressed and angry at minimum most of the time. I remember her either being mad or drunk almost every day. Back then, there didn't seem to be another side to her.

Afraid of causing my parents to fight, I quietly played in a corner of the living room with dolls or games so she wouldn't get mad. Riddled with fear, I thought if I was good enough and quiet enough, she would be pleased with me. I don't recall a time when Mom and Dad were kind to each other. They yelled at each other, called each other nasty names and never spoke with love or kindness toward each other. I carried a sense of dread with me most of the time as a little girl. After Mom left, there was still no peace in the house, at least not for me. It only brought more internal turmoil. I constantly worried about Mom. I wondered about her safety. I wrote her letters every week so she would know how much I loved her and missed her. I was crushed she no longer lived with us and sad most of the time without her. But most of all, I didn't want Mom to stop loving me, if she still did.

My parents' relationship was unhealthy and they both wanted control of every situation. What I didn't know back then, was that Dad tried to keep Mom from seeing us many times. His argument was that we weren't safe with her because of her alcohol abuse. I suppose a power struggle ensued and my sisters and I were the pawns. In their dysfunction, I don't think they had any idea how their behavior negatively affected us. My thoughts were always the same: *How could Mom leave us? Did she not love us anymore? Did she miss me at all? Why is Dad so mad at Mom all the time?*

Disturbing questions ran through my mind constantly, yet remained unanswered. Healthy communication was not a common activity in our family. Although there was a huge, white elephant in the room called alcoholism, no one talked about it--

ever. Everyone walked around on eggshells as if it didn't exist and nothing got explained or resolved. Therefore, I accepted that as the normal way of dealing with my emotions and feelings. Ignore or stuff them, but *never* talk about them.

After Mom left, Dad raised us three girls with help from our aunts. I can only imagine the burden of raising three girls; certainly it must have been an extremely daunting task for him. In the 1970s, divorce was much less accepted and the idea of children staying with their father instead of their mother was out of the ordinary. This was another reason I felt like a misfit around my friends. Honestly, I have no idea how Dad accomplished all he did, working full time while raising us girls.

From the time I was seven until about age ten, Mom and I saw each other on an irregular basis, but I was thankful to see her at all. I craved her love and approval. She wasn't very affectionate and I perceived her lack of affection as how she felt about me personally. I feared she didn't love me anymore and maybe thought I had something to do with Dad kicking her out. I tried as hard as I could to be the perfect child when we were together. I told her repeatedly how much I loved her and missed her, in the desperate hope of winning her affection.

She and Dad barely spoke to one another when they were in the same room, which, thankfully, was a rare occasion. Nervousness consumed me the few times they were around each other. I constantly picked at and bit my fingernails. The fear of an argument breaking out was always in the back of my mind even though secretly, I wanted them to get back together. If they got back together, surely my life would be normal again. Although, I had no idea what normal meant.

When I was ten years old, I was heartbroken at the thought of Dad remarrying. Even though I had my own bedroom, I preferred to sleep in Dad's room in his huge, king-sized bed. I was afraid of the dark and felt more secure in Dad's room. When Dad sat Tanya, Terri and me down to tell us he was going to marry, the first question that came out of my mouth was, "But Dad, where am I going to sleep?" Of course he replied, "Your room," but that didn't provide any relief. I was always the baby of the family and with six years between Terri and me, I usually got my way. But not this time. I didn't want to sleep in my own room and certainly didn't want to get kicked out of Dad's life like Mom had been years before.

With my home life interrupted, I wanted to run away and live with Mom, who was now remarried too. I missed having Dad all to myself. Jealousy crept into my heart concerning his relationship with his new wife, Peggy. I also had to share his attention with my new stepsister, LeAnna, and soon after, Sam, my new baby brother. This entirely new family situation was quite difficult to adjust to and my territory felt threatened every day. Since we were a family that never talked, none of our step family issues got resolved. Layer upon layer, insecurities, fear, and jealousy became my cloak.

When I was eleven, I attended church camp at Hidden Falls Ranch with some cousins and my step-sister. We certainly weren't a religious family and I'm sure our parents were probably looking for a place to send us off for a week during the summer. Church camp was a great option.

I figured out that the goal at camp was to accept Jesus into my heart and be saved. Because I knew this was expected, dutifully, I said the sinner's prayer and asked Jesus to come into my heart. I didn't understand what that meant at the time, but I did believe that's what was expected of me and I knew how to do what was expected. Many of the other campers had already done this and I wanted to fit in with them. Everything my counselor said about Jesus sounded so good to me at the time. Afterward, she and I walked down to the big, metal bell and I rang it as loud as I could. All the campers heard the bell when someone got saved. This was the sound of ultimate achievement for me.

At the time, I didn't understand the importance of being saved, but I now thank God for that night. He marked me as His and nothing could change that. It took several years and many wrong paths for me to realize the impact that night would have on my life.

Of course, when I got back home from camp, life returned to its normal state, which meant Jesus wasn't a frequent guest in our home, although everyone claimed to believe in God. I think we believed in God because everyone else did. No one in my family had a personal relationship with Jesus. He was like an acquaintance, but certainly not a friend. Even with my camp experience, I still didn't develop an intimate relationship with Him myself.

My family never prayed before meals, or spoke about God, although I did hear His name taken in vain many times. My perception of God was much like a dictator who ruled over me. The Bible was a set of laws to live by, not that I ever could. Deep inside, I still believed that Mom left because I was bad and God was punishing me for that. God was aloof to me; distant and cold. It was so difficult for me to grasp the idea that God sent His Son, Jesus to the cross to die for my sins. Why? I thought. I'm a terrible person, why would You do that, God?

Occasionally, throughout my teenage years, I attended church with friends and their families. I wanted to believe there was some good in me and that Jesus really died to save me from my sins. Yet, the teachings I heard back then never took root deep enough to withstand the weeds of the negative images I had of myself. They choked out the truth.

Although I put Jesus on a shelf, He never let go of me. Over the years, there were brief moments that I prayed and felt close to Jesus, but they never lasted. I had not learned yet, that unlike people, thankfully, Jesus never 'unfriends' us.

# Chapter Four

## *No Place to Call Home*

February 7, 1981, was a brisk, winter Saturday. I remember it well. Around 9:00 in the morning, my girlfriend, Bonnie, called and asked me to ride to a nearby town with her. That seemed like a good reason to get out of our little hometown of Sunray, Texas and see a change of scenery. With a population of only 1500, any excuse was good enough. The only thing between me and a trip to Dumas, the next town over, was to ask Dad for permission, something that in my mind compared to climbing Mt. Everest. I had a healthy amount of fear and reverence for Dad—so much so, that it might take me hours to get enough courage to ask his permission to do anything. He never beat me, but when he yelled or was disappointed with me, I was crushed. So, for him to tell me "no" was just another form of rejection that I couldn't endure.

I finally got my nerve up and went back to his bedroom where he watched TV and sat down in the chair beside his bed, the 'hot seat' as I referred to it. As he surfed through the channels on the TV, he came across a fashion show, full of towering models sauntering down the long, narrow runway.

I said, "Dad, stop just a second. I want to do that someday. I want to model on a runway."

"Well, that's okay for a time, but you need to have something else to fall back on, Honey. You should study to be a secretary or something. You can't model forever," Dad advised.

I agreed with him and we shared some small talk. The entire scene was so uncommon; having a conversation about my future with Dad. I never talked about my future with Dad and I was shocked he seemed interested. He was unusually chatty that morning and I remember feeling closer to him than I ever had, just from that one conversation. I sat quietly for another ten or fifteen minutes. Then, with my heart beating faster and faster, I got the courage up to ask if I could ride to Dumas with my friend, Bonnie.

Holding my breath, awaiting the anticipated "no," his response surprised me. "Sure, Honey, just be careful."

*What did he just say?* I was so excited he said yes and I didn't have to explain why, or how or anything else. He said yes! I couldn't believe it!

I hugged his neck, "Thank you Dad. We'll be careful!" and with a spring in my step, ran on my way before he changed his mind.

My friend, Bonnie and I traveled seventeen miles to Dumas to do nothing really, but get out of Sunray for a while. We stopped and got a soft drink and window shopped, visiting about boys the entire time. It was around lunch time when I saw my older sister, Tanya and my stepsister, LeAnna driving through town. I wondered what they were doing in Dumas, when they turned around and were behind us, flagging us to pull over. Bonnie and I were near the hospital so we pulled into the emergency room parking lot. Before Tanya could get out of the car, LeAnna jumped out and ran to my window and exclaimed, "Dad's dead!"

*What did she just say?* I couldn't believe what I heard, so I asked, "What?"

Again, LeAnna said, "Dad's dead!" By this time, I was crying and Tanya made it to me and held me. In a matter of a few seconds, my life changed forever. I cried hysterically and was in shock as well. I closed my eyes and envisioned Dad and I sitting in his room just a few hours before, talking about my future, and now, I hear he's dead? *Just like that? This can not be. Dad took care of me. Who was going to take care of me?*

It seemed within the course of a few minutes, thousands of feelings and thoughts rushed through my mind at mach speed. I couldn't control them. The most important person in my life, my rock, was gone. I would never have another conversation with Dad again. The all-powerful security that his presence provided me was gone, forever. *How on Earth will I live without Dad?*

Sorrow covered me like a heavy blanket that I couldn't get out from under. I wanted my dad. I felt vulnerable now with him gone and there was no one to take care of my affairs. Dad always took care of me and Peggy took care of LeAnna, that's just the way it was. In my mind, Peggy was not capable of taking care of me, only Dad was.

I repeatedly thought, "I don't want to be here . . . I don't want to live without Dad. I don't think I can live without Dad." After aimlessly driving around Sunray that evening with my cousin, I knew it was time to go home.

*Home. Where was home, now?* A sick feeling welled up inside me at the thought of going back to my house, knowing Dad was not there. I called Peggy and told her I wanted to spend the night at my cousin's. Despite the late hour, but considering the events of the day, she agreed. The next few days after Dad died are a blur.

Without Dad, I was quite lost. Mom left when I was seven, Dad died when I was fifteen. A sense of having no roots eroded my heart. I already felt like a misfit from Mom leaving, now I certainly knew I belonged nowhere. My fears escalated as I wondered what was going to happen to me. Inside, I felt abandoned by both Mom and Dad and helpless all at the same time. I had no idea how I was going to function without Dad to take care of me. I was lost without his security and presence. A few times, the thought of dying flitted through my mind. I really didn't think I would kill myself, but I wasn't sure how I could live without Dad. The truth was, I was too afraid of death to hurt myself, but that didn't stop me from thinking about it.

With rejection and abandonment weighing in heavily, I continued to think there was something inherently wrong with me. All these events gave me a sense of being punished for something. *I must be so bad; that's why Mom left and Dad died.* That was the rationale in my head. I believed my punishment came directly from God, which did not help improve our already shallow relationship.

Peggy decided to move LeAnna and Sam closer to her family in East Texas, so I moved in with my aunt, uncle and cousins. I don't remember how that decision was made, but I knew I didn't want to go with Peggy. Although, whether being uprooted to move a hundred miles away, or two blocks away, the effects are similar. My sense of belonging slowly washed away with every box I packed. I belonged with my dad. *Would I fit in at my aunt and uncle's house? Do they really want me to move in?*

I took up residence in their guest room, but there wasn't space for all of my belongings. Most of my things were stored in various family member's attics. What could fit in my new room were my most needed possessions: clothes, shoes, and a few pictures. I hung on to a couple of my favorite stuffed animals. I couldn't bear to let go of everything and clung to anything that gave me comfort from living with my dad. I missed him so much, I ached inside. Yet, as usual, I stuffed those feelings deep inside the corners of my soul.

As thoughtful as it was for my aunt and uncle to allow me to come live with them, it wasn't home. My dad was gone forever and the hole left in my heart from his loss couldn't be filled. My sisters, Tanya and Terri were living in Amarillo and Midland, respectively and I didn't see them much during the next few years. Mom came around more and eventually married a wonderful man from Dumas. A few years later, they moved back to my hometown of Sunray. I enjoyed having Mom back in my life and in closer proximity; however, her alcoholism had escalated over the years. It was quite difficult to get close to Mom with her disease in full force. When Mom was sober, she was pensive and agitated and difficult to talk to. When she was intoxicated, she was much more talkative, but sometimes it turned into anger. Those conversations were never fun and left me feeling unworthy and like a failure.

It was during this time, after Dad's death, that I experimented more with alcohol. My self-esteem was at an all-time low and I didn't feel I had the right to any of my feelings, especially my anger. I was still angry that Mom left me and she refused to quit drinking. I was angry that Dad was dead; and I was angry that I lived with an aunt and uncle who were in a legal battle with my sister and I felt like a misfit. I wanted to have a close relationship with Mom, as any daughter would, but it was impossible with her drinking. She didn't seem interested in developing a close relationship, so it continued on the surface, as usual.

Because I didn't feel I had the right to be angry with anyone, I drank to numb the pain and the anger. The numbing effects of alcohol were exactly what I needed to ease the internal pain and insecurities I suffered. As an insecure child from an early age, I was never able to express my feelings well. I wanted people around me to be pleased with me at all times. When Mom got angry, I reverted to that scared little seven year old who heard Dad and her argue. Even as a teenager, I was riddled with nervousness, fear and anxiety. I remember playing softball and never taking a swing for fear I'd miss. Same thing happened in basketball. During the games, I never shot the ball for fear I'd miss. I was paralyzed with fear.

Compounding my already insecure state was the feeling that I never measured up to anyone's expectations. More than anything,

I wanted to be loved unconditionally by my aunt and feel as if I belonged in her home. I was desperate for a "mother's love." But no matter how hard I tried to obtain unconditional love, I felt increasingly more like a burden, which exaggerated my self-esteem issues. I was in a state of internal turmoil during those years because of the legal battles between my loved ones following Dad's death. I felt like I was in the middle of a tug-o-war battle. It seemed, no matter what I did, I was going to hurt someone. I didn't understand all the complexities of the legal battle within my family, but from my perspective, it was a no-win situation for me.

My junior year in high school, I dated a guy who was three years my senior. My dad would not have approved of me dating him and I know now it was a manifestation of my rebellion and feeling helpless in my situation. I believed I was in love even though our relationship mirrored that of Mom and Dad's. Fight, break up, get back together, repeat.

The arguments escalated when alcohol was involved and unfortunately, that became more frequent. I wanted to belong somewhere so badly that I clung to this unhealthy relationship for years. It didn't matter that we didn't get along all the time, I couldn't let go and face the feeling of abandonment again. I was willing to succumb to an unhealthy situation to forego being alone.

In an effort to please everyone from Midland to Sunray, I attended Texas Tech University the summer after I graduated. I arrived in Lubbock, Texas, a few days before summer classes began. I cried the entire trip to Lubbock. I was so confused about who I was, what I was doing and, at the core of all this, I needed to please my family. The last few years of grief, abandonment and turmoil had such a devastating effect on me that I was afraid of my own shadow. I'd never learned how to express my feelings and was reluctant to say anything for fear of someone being displeased or disappointed with me.

I found myself in a dormitory with several sorority girls who didn't have a problem with self-confidence like I did. Having any conversation with them caused me to feel even more insecure. I knew I didn't belong there, but I was trying to keep the peace in my family and please everyone. I literally walked around as if I was on egg shells all the time. My heart raced all day and I was as nervous as a cat! Anxiousness overshadowed every other feeling I had.

Let me give you an example of how nervous and insecure I was. My first day at Texas Tech, I unloaded a couple of boxes from my car and proceeded to the elevator in the dorm up to my floor. A couple of really confident sorority girls were on the elevator with me. As they laughed and giggled with one another, I wanted to disappear in my despair. When the doors opened, directly across from the elevator was a mirrored wall. Walking with my head downcast, I caught a glimpse of my image in the mirror and thought I was about to walk right into someone! Mind you, I was only a couple of inches away from the mirror.

"Oh, I'm sorry," I exclaimed. Only it was ME in the mirror. Knowing the sorority girls saw this, I turned fire-engine red. Embarrassed and humiliated, I laughed a nervous laugh and took off to my room. Now, that is the definition of literally being afraid of one's own shadow.

I cried off and on throughout the next three days and even had suicidal thoughts. I truly wanted to die to escape the turmoil I was in. Pain is something we all want to avoid, and some of us cope better than others. At this point, I was not coping well at all.

On the third day, I attended an English class and couldn't concentrate on the instructor's lecture for any length of time. My thoughts were consumed with escaping my pain. I couldn't handle the pressure any longer and I packed up and drove back home. Relief emerged the closer I got to home, even though I felt like a total failure. This insecure, smalltown girl was not able to cope or handle the large campus. I certainly believe that experience was the precursor for many similar events throughout my life. To please others, I often did what I thought they wanted, only to discover, it wasn't right for me at all. During this time, I honed the art of people-pleasing, approval-seeking and perfectionism, not realizing those coping skills would someday cause my demise.

After I returned home with my tail between my legs, I decided to attend West Texas State University in the fall. It was a much smaller campus and closer to home. And there was one particular perk that undoubtedly appealed to me: a lot less people. There was still some freedom living one hundred miles away from home and all the pain associated with it and my family situation. However, with all that freedom, came the emotional baggage I'd toted around for years.

To that point in my life, there were no positive examples of healthy ways to cope with difficult situations. Not surprisingly, I chose what I had seen in the past from my parents. So I did what came natural: abused alcohol, stuffed my emotions and denied the pain that suffocated me.

Another form of self-abuse I experimented with at college was binging and purging both food and alcohol. With alcohol, I purged so I could drink more and continue to party and avoid the emotional pain I held so deeply within my soul. With food, I binged and purged as a way to have some control over my life that was so out of control. My aunt and uncle paid for my college tuition and I was so grateful they did, but I continued to pressure myself to perform as I sought their approval. My insecurity, lack of confidence and the fear of failure plagued me. No matter what I did, I could not avoid the horrible way I felt for more than a few hours of partying. The relief was always short-lived.

Most people go to college to graduate; I went to escape. I certainly didn't recognize the benefit a four year college education could give me, nor did I care. While at college, I relished the freedom to do what I wanted, when I wanted. I'd never had that kind of freedom before in my life.

My first semester reflected my carefree behavior with a 1.4 GPA. That GPA was a sign of where I was emotionally in my life—clueless, reckless and spinning out of control. As usual my performance left me shocked and discouraged with such a low grade. I felt like such a failure, especially after making A's and B's in high school. I had no idea my lifestyle could destroy my GPA. Although disappointed with my grades, my aunt and uncle continued to pay for my college tuition. That was certainly a wake-up call. I never made a GPA that low again and I studied more to bring my grades up.

Mom continued to encourage me to graduate from college harping, "You don't need a man to take care of you." My heart suspected that her motivation came from years of anger at Dad and not purely to encourage me for my own good. Mom probably didn't want me to make the same mistakes she'd made. I longed for her to sincerely be concerned about me from a place of love, not anger. Despite Mom's continual influence, deep down, I desired a loving husband and a place to belong much more than I did a degree or career. I never voiced that to her because I feared her disappointment. In fact, I never voiced that to anyone.

The constant conflict in the most pivotal relationships in my life continued to erode my self-image, confidence and any dreams I might have. It seemed everyone else controlled my destiny. Some days, it was all I could do to survive. I learned early on to be quiet, never express my emotions and do all I could to please others to keep the peace. One of the worst side effects I encountered to my debilitating people-pleasing behavior was the lack of any boundaries. Because I had no idea who I was, I would completely lose myself in any relationship in an effort to please the other person. Emotionally, I was in shambles and this became my normal cycle of behavior for the next twenty years.

The depth of the hole in my heart left from Dad's death was unable to be filled no matter how I tried – and boy, did I try! Drugs, alcohol, promiscuity, materialism, attending church, attending bars - it didn't matter what it was; nothing filled the hole. The emptiness inside me was unbearable at times. I felt like a feather floating through the air with no destination, no place to land and, definitely, no place to belong.

Frequently, I felt like a little seven year old girl trapped in a grown woman's body; the same little girl I was when Mom left me. I've heard that people get emotionally stuck at the age of their earliest trauma. I coped with life through the eyes of a broken little seven year old. I knew something was wrong with me and hated the way I felt in relationships. I was inconsistent, jealous and threatened all the time. I was tired of walking around with no confidence, yet I had no idea how to act different, or more importantly, how to *be* different. I didn't like who I was, but no matter what I tried, I could not get away from myself. I felt like a crazy cat going around in circles, chasing her tail, not realizing it's *her* tail!

# Chapter
## Five
*Reckless Rebellion*

After my first year of college, Mom was diagnosed with breast cancer. Again, my already shaky world trembled. Mom and I were never that close, yet she was still my mom and I longed to have a mother-daughter relationship like my other girlfriends had with their moms, but that was simply not a possibility. Mom continued to drink heavily and when she got the cancer diagnosis, her years of hidden anger exploded to the surface like a volcano. In my opinion, most people abuse alcohol because they don't want to deal with their pain from past hurts. Mom loved Dad, but also hated him. He was gone now, but the issues she had with him for the past twenty-plus years were never resolved and it seemed that was the source of most of her anger and pain. Dealing with Mom's disease of cancer coupled with her alcoholism was extremely difficult for me. She was mad about everything. When she got the diagnosis of cancer, she moved through the first stage of grief, but then focused exclusively on her prognosis and remained stuck in the angry phase. My heart broke to see her in such emotional and physical agony as she endured the difficult chemotherapy and radiation treatments. My helplessness added to my agony. At my young age of nineteen, I could not fathom the loss of another parent.

For the next three years Mom underwent various treatments for the cancer while I tried to focus on school with lackluster results. Shortly after the third anniversary of her diagnosis, it appeared the cancer was not responding positively. Even through all of this, Mom had to be in control of everything. Knowing the end was near, she was on a mission to plan her funeral arrangements completely, down to the songs played, and design the pamphlet given out at her memorial service.

An upwelling of extreme anger rose within when she talked about her memorial service to my sister, Tanya, and me. Inside, I felt I was the one dying. Part of me knew she would not beat cancer, but another part of me was in denial and believed that there was no way God would take her too.

In August, 1987, no one was more shocked than I was that I graduated from West Texas State University. When I set off to attend college, the idea of graduating was never on my radar. No one in our family had graduated from college and the idea that I might be the first seemed impossible. Yet, here I was receiving my diploma. Even after such an accomplishment, I realized very little had changed in my world and neither had I. I was still the same fearful, insecure little girl I was at age seven. I wanted to please all of the people in my life, but deep down I knew I would fail. I protected myself by engaging in self-destructive behaviors and denial. I felt it was my responsibility to fix everyone else, but that simply was not realistic, so when it didn't happen it just compounded my guilt and sense of failure.

A few weeks after I graduated from college, Mom's condition deteriorated quickly. Although I still had unresolved issues with my mom, I wanted to spend time with her in the last stages of her life. I sometime daydreamed that she and I would have that special mother-daughter talk and I could be at peace, once and for all.

I packed up and went home to help take care of her. Soon after I arrived, Mom said, "Dawn, I don't want any of my family to have to take care of me after I lose my faculties, so I've arranged to be admitted into St. Anthony's Hospice when that happens." Internally, I was devastated when she said that. She knew it wouldn't be long and, because of her controlling nature, she wanted everything done her way, even death. I still didn't want to deal with the reality that she would not beat cancer. 'Not dealing' was how I'd stumbled through life so far and I didn't see any changes on the horizon.

Caring for Mom was odd for me. I knew she had regrets, but her pride wouldn't allow her to admit any fault or seek any sort of resolution. It seemed she was still angry about everything. I suspected she was most angry with herself. So much time had been wasted and she wasn't going to get any more. My heart ached for her and the life of regret she'd lived. I had always taken the sympathetic role toward Mom, despite my unresolved anger with her for abandoning me years ago. She was the 'underdog' between her and Dad in my opinion, and I always had a soft spot for the underdog.

While at Mom's modest home, I slept on the couch in the living room. Mom slept in the guest room which was only a door away from me. Her pain worsened every day and she withdrew inside herself.

The last breath of summer was soon gone and the crisp air of fall moved in. Early on November 9th, 1987, a loud thud awoke me. Something had hit the ground hard. I jumped up and ran into the bedroom and found Mom lying on the floor. I went to her and she was trying to get up, but couldn't. She seemed disoriented and confused as she looked at me and asked, "What happened?"

"You fell Mom. Let me help you up to the bed," I said.

I grabbed her under her thin, frail arms and pulled her to her feet guiding her back to the bed. She had no idea what happened. *It's time.* Oh, how I dreaded this day. I was torn between accepting the fact that the end was near, yet I wanted Mom to be out of pain and to respect her wishes.

My aunt and cousin came over in their van a short time later and we loaded Mom in the back part on a pallet of blankets to transport her as we drove her to Hospice. It was one of the saddest sights I'd ever seen. Mom wasn't aware of her surroundings anymore and didn't recognize anyone. Overnight, Mom's health had spiraled downward and I knew this was it. I could hardly take it in; my strong-willed, feminist Mom, lying there helpless and frail, dying right before my eyes.

The hour and a half ride to Hospice seemed like an eternity. I sat in the middle seat of the van and quietly wept at the thought of how near her death was. I couldn't believe this was happening again and I was about to lose my only parent. My heart was shattered at that thought. *God, why are You doing this? Is it me? Tell me, is it ME?*

We arrived at Hospice and she was admitted to her room quickly, since she had pre-admitted herself several weeks prior. Within minutes the nurses allowed us to come in and see her. They had her on a morphine drip and she rested well. The nurse said her pain level was minimal, which comforted me. The room was quiet and dark - great for resting contently. For the first time in my life, She seemed at peace. *Mom, I wish you could have felt this way before now.*

J.B., Mom's husband, slept in a recliner in her room and I slept on the couch in the Great Room at Hospice. I was so thankful the staff allowed me to do that. I could not leave Hospice for fear I'd miss if she woke up, or God forbid, passed away. That first night, I reminisced about Mom's life. Her unique, feminist personality gave her many opportunities to adventures many women of her time would never have even tried.

She took flying lessons and flew her first solo flight at the Sunray Airport. She got her real estate license, and worked to provide for herself after she and Dad divorced. She also had a sense of style on a shoestring budget like no other woman I knew. Her tall, slender frame was always dressed to the nines and looked like a million bucks. Her style was classic and traditional and she wore it well. If she said it once, she said it a thousand times, "Dawn, don't EVER wear white shoes—EVER!" (Not even after Easter). After all these years, I remember it like she said it yesterday and, to this day, I do not own a pair of white dress shoes!

Mom had a fabulous green thumb and loved gardening. Wherever she lived, there were always beautiful flowers around. She surrounded herself with beautiful things and I loved that about her. I always believed she was a good, kind person underneath the alcoholism and I longed for a relationship with that person. Yet as I watched her die, I realized that dream would never come true.

Several days went by in Hospice and Mom rested peacefully. I asked God, "Why are You doing this? What is the point of her lying there day after day, never waking up?" Moments after I prayed that internal prayer, I felt guilty for even asking God such a thing. I didn't want Mom to die, but I didn't want her to lie there helpless and lifeless either. The internal conflict continued in my heart and I wrestled with every feeling that arose.

When my sister, Terri, arrived, she held Mom's hand and told her how much she loved her. They always had the most tumultuous relationship of all of us girls. A few times when Terri went into Mom's room, Mom awoke slightly and acted as if she wanted to say something and finally, on that seventh day while Terri held her hand, Mom slightly opened her eyes and in barely a whisper said, "I'm so sorry." Those were the last words Mom ever spoke. I am so thankful she spoke them to Terri; it needed to be said.

At 3:00 in the morning, J.B. woke me and softly said that Mom was gone. I jumped up and ran into her room, thinking he might be wrong. When I arrived, I knew at first glance, she was gone. Her eyes were closed with no furrow between her brows, and her mouth had the slightest grin across it. A smile you might see on someone who was at peace where they were. After all the years of struggle, Mom finally seemed to reach a place of rest. *Finally*.

A heavy burden of guilt rushed over me for asking God just the day before, why He allowed Mom to lie there lifeless. I wanted to take all of that back and see her again, alive. Tears burst from my eyes because I knew I couldn't take it back. Nothing was going to bring her back.

Waves of emotions rolled through me like a rollercoaster that wouldn't stop. I railed at God. *Why did You take her? Why did You take both of them?* Fear and anger rose up inside me. The finality of her death now made me fear life without either of my parents. I also realized there would never be a chance to have the relationship I'd always desired to have with Mom. Anger welled up again about her abandoning me all those years ago. I missed her; I loved her and I was mad at her; all at the same time. The emotions and thoughts that flooded my mind overwhelmed me. I didn't know how to feel or what was appropriate. As usual, I doubted myself and didn't believe I could even grieve correctly.

The two people that brought me into this world were gone. *Forever*. I was terrified of life from that perspective and paralyzed with fear. There was no one left to defend, protect or love me, I thought. I had my two sisters, but they were experiencing their own emotional rollercoasters and were hardly able to take on my problems or concerns. After Dad's death, we all scattered and tried to survive, which was a feat everyday of our lives.

The next few days were a foggy blur. Friends called and came over and extended their sympathies. Cards came with encouraging thoughts of prayers and support. All very much appreciated, but it was unable to fill the enormous hole in my heart that seemed to grow deeper and deeper now with Mom's death on top of Dad's.

Mom's memorial service was exactly as she planned. She arranged for each song played on a cassette player that was listed on the pamphlet, which she designed herself. It had everything on it except the day she died—the one thing she had no control over, which I'm sure irritated her to no end. The last song played at her service was *My Way* by Elvis Presley. As the words hung in the air at the end of the service: "I did it my way," a smile crossed my face as I remembered Mom as the courageous, feisty woman she was. She got the last word, even if she had to die to do it.

At her request, her ashes were strewn over the Sunray Airport. It was the location of her first solo flight, which in her eyes was her most aspiring accomplishment. She chose for all of us to have a wake at her house, although she was never Catholic. Honestly, I believe she wanted us to celebrate her life and the only way she knew how to do that was with a liberal supply of alcohol. Her wet bar was completely stocked—another detail she took care of before her demise. Since I wanted to respect Mom's wishes, I drank with gusto. My heart was so broken by this time and my emotions so raw, that the idea of numbing that pain was the best plan I could think of. I got extremely intoxicated that night, as if hoping to obliterate the past several years of my life. I didn't want to feel anything. I accomplished that objective at least until I awoke the next morning. *Ouch.* I paid with a relentless headache.

The physical pain of my hangover was no match for the broken heart in my chest. My family was now dismantled in a permanent way. I was officially an orphan. *Where on Earth do I belong? There's no one left to love me? Where do I go from here? Will my life ever get any easier?*

At this point in my life, I was miserable. To add to my misery, I was confused, grieving, angry, and emotionally broken into a thousand pieces. I had no idea how I would face that big world out there without any roots. With both my parents dead, I had absolutely no grounding. I literally did not belong anywhere or to anyone. Yes, I still had two sisters, but they weren't my parents. They didn't bring me into this world and they had no responsibility for me. In fact, all three of us were on our own in the great big world. As much pain as I was in, they were too. At the time, we were too weak to help each other because we all carried such heavy emotional baggage and issues from our past. The three of us were trying to survive with none of us doing a very good job, either.

Running was a typical escape mechanism of mine that seemed to be the answer. Even if it gave some temporary relief, it always proved to be the wrong move in the end. While faced with the fear of being all alone, I ran to the Dallas-Fort Worth area in an attempt to get lost in the big city.

With $3,300 in my pocket, I packed up and moved to the city to begin a new chapter in my life that I believed would bring some joy and happiness. I desired a reprieve from the relentless sadness my hometown held for me. As insecure and unconfident as I was, I actually went through with the move. Desperately miserable in my own skin, I thought a geographical change would magically make my life so much better. What a lie that turned out to be. Changing one's geographical location does not change one's heart.

If I felt I didn't belong in my hometown because of the death of my parents, I absolutely knew I didn't belong in the big city. While I lived in the DFW area, I continued my search to fill the gaping hole in my heart. I was so lost, confused and desperate. As many people do, I tried to fill the hole with all the wrong ingredients. For the first time in my life, I tried marijuana, completely succumbing to peer pressure. I'd certainly done my share of drinking over the past ten years, but now I was exposed to much more sophisticated, recreational drugs I'd never seen. Drugs were readily available here as they had not been in my small home town. I quickly learned that the high from these drugs came at a steep price, not only financially, but emotionally as well. It brought so much shame and guilt because deep down, I knew what I was doing was wrong, but I was desperate to avoid my own pain. I've learned that desperate people do desperate things and *I was one desperate person.* I accomplished temporary relief while I disconnected from my anguish, but once the high was over, reality crashed back in with a force and carried even more guilt. I was searching long and hard for a way to fit in; a place to belong. It didn't matter where I was: at work, at a nightclub, in a church or with a boyfriend, I never seemed to quite fit in. I didn't feel I belonged to anyone, anywhere. When a person is that lost, they are susceptible to influences that might never have interested them in the past. It didn't take much for me to be persuaded to do anything that offered a temporary reprieve.

The few years I lived in the DFW area were undeniably the most rebellious years I ever experienced. I went through life with reckless abandon because deep down, I felt I had nothing to live for--not even myself. I can remember many mornings after partying how depressed and suicidal I felt. I just wanted to die. Guilt, shame and condemnation became my Morning Greeters and maintained perfect attendance. It didn't take long for me to figure out I could not keep using drugs and continue to function. I understand how so many get addicted and are unable to stop abusing them.

I was certainly no stranger to addiction; I'd seen its effects over the course of Mom's life. All the anger, fear, rejection and abandonment issues I continued to harbor manifested in my destructive actions. My goal was to not feel the way I felt. Drugs weren't my problem; it was my inability to deal with my emotions in a healthy way. Pain was my problem and by this point, it was a huge problem. Since I'd never learned to talk about my feelings, they remained suppressed deep inside me, but that didn't make them go away. That's what the drugs and alcohol accomplished, at least, temporarily.

*Compulsive* is defined as resulting from or relating to an irresistible urge, especially one that is against one's conscious wishes. Addictions come in many different forms. Usually, if you add the word "compulsive" to anything, it can become an addiction; for example, compulsive eating, compulsive shopping, compulsive gambling, compulsive exercising. Do you see my point? No matter what the compulsion is, it controls you. It takes over your thoughts and your actions; it's as if it owns your soul. Until one decides to address their pain and surrender their compulsive behavior, it will always control them.

To my benefit, in 1991, my sister, Terri, encouraged me to attend a seminar conducted by Dr. Phil McGraw and his father. It was a confidence building seminar and she believed I could gain greatly from attending. For some time, I scoffed at her attempts to persuade me to attend the seminar, but after several unhealthy, failed relationships, I realized I had nothing to lose.

Through that self-help seminar, I finally came out of my shell and experienced life without rebellion, alcohol, or drugs. I touched on my pain and didn't die from the experience, which was a great start. Even the debilitating fear seemed much less prevalent. I walked away from the last meeting with more confidence than I'd ever exhibited in my life. I felt I'd dropped a ton of baggage from my past and was able to move forward. I continued to stay involved with the seminar and volunteered when able. I gained a new circle of friends that grew larger with each weekend. I tasted hope for the first time in my life. The high continued for several months, but as always with external sources, it was only a temporary fix. One thing I knew for sure was that I needed to remove myself from the job I'd had for the past year and the friends I'd made there. The temptation to drink and use drugs remained, and I thought a change in scenery would help.

I obtained a new job only to find the same situation awaited me there as well. Even though I touched on my pain during that seminar, I was nowhere near healed. It was a quick fix for me, but didn't go deep enough to the root. I certainly had more confidence than ever before, but I still didn't have all the tools necessary to secure my happiness, joy and fulfillment. It wasn't long before I was in the same situation with a co-worker, drinking and partying and living immorally. Frustrated with my inconsistent behavior, I turned my anger inward. I was convinced there was something terribly wrong with me and I would never 'get it.' Depression was the result of that anger and it, of course, went untreated.

For the next five years, I made geographical moves, took new jobs, went to church, went to the bar and continued living an inconsistent life. The internal battle continued as I tried to make good decisions, but never had the tools to maintain them consistently. I went through periods of depression as my anger toward myself worsened because of my lack of success at living a prosperous and healthy life. I ran to the church believing I needed God, but wasn't ready to surrender my entire life to Him. My deep desire to control everything even spilled over into that relationship. I didn't believe God could handle my life entirely on His own, so I kept my hands in the mix. A half-surrendered life only reaps half the benefits, if that much. I wanted to be a good person and sometimes was, but the worldly desires of my flesh won out every time.

The underlying force that motivated my behaviors came from a deep desire to belong somewhere and to someone. Since my parents' death, I lived life from an orphan mindset. It was difficult for me to allow anyone to get too close because I feared abandonment; yet the one thing I desired more than anything was to be close to someone! It didn't make sense, yet that is how I lived life for many years.

Finally, in 1996, the desire to belong to someone overrode the fear of abandonment and I married for the first time at the age of thirty. I thought I was old enough by then to know who would make a great husband for me and we married after dating four months. Although I was thirty years old, emotionally, I was still a broken-hearted little girl, searching for someone to make everything all right.

I was so emotionally unhealthy and that rendered me unable to connect on any level of intimacy. Our marriage had struggles beyond our ability to resolve. I related to my husband just as I did towards my dad—a fearful, emotionally immature little girl. I was unable to express my feelings or communicate my needs and made horrible choices out of my inability to make our marriage the perfect fantasy I'd dreamed of. I thought if I could change him, our marriage would be perfect. What a lie we tell ourselves, many times to avoid changing the very things in us that prevent a successful relationship. It seemed easier to point the finger at him than to actually look inside myself and deal with my own pain. Pride keeps our blinders on.

After six years, that marriage ended in an extremely difficult divorce. At times, the pain was more excruciating than losing both my parents. I never thought I'd have more pain than that, but I was wrong. We never had children and I thank God. I couldn't imagine how much more painful a divorce would be if children were involved. We had Shorty, my miniature dachshund, and it was difficult enough for us to reach an agreement about her. It broke my heart to take her away from my ex-husband because I knew how much he loved her too. I can only guess how much more difficult that would be with children?

The pain I felt from the guilt, shame and condemnation was so intense, I could hardly stand it some days. As my life took on a new persona as a divorced woman, I felt shame from failing miserably at my marriage. It seemed the word DIVORCED was tattooed on my forehead and everyone looked at me as a failure. I made mistakes that I never dreamed I would and wished I could take them all back, but I couldn't. The regret from the pain I caused was overwhelming at times and it seemed the only thing that gave me any relief, albeit temporary, was to drown my sorrow in alcohol.

Many mornings, I awoke to find shame and condemnation waiting for me at the edge of my thoughts. The first thing I did was stuff them down as far as I could, and put on my happy face to get through the day. Then, most evenings after work, I assembled at the bar with friends and subsequently diluted that pain with the next drink. I'd momentarily forget about all my mistakes, laugh with my friends and enjoy a reprieve from an overwhelming sense of failure. The next morning started the vicious cycle all over again. I wondered if life was ever going to get better. I'd made a mess of it thus far and from what I could tell, nothing was going to change in the near future.

There was one feeling I had that could not be denied. In the quietest moments, I felt a tug at my heart and sensed it was God. My fear of His disappointment kept me from doing an about face and running into His arms. I knew I was a failure on so many levels and believed He was sick and tired of me running to Him on *my* selfish terms. Even though I wanted what Godly people had, such as peace, joy, and contentment; I didn't understand how to get it and keep it.

*What if I fail You again? I've been so inconsistent all my life; I don't trust myself.* I believed His forgiveness was for others, but not for a wretch like me. As far as I could surmise, I was bad all my life. Nothing ever stuck with me and there was no reason to think that what others had was something I could have too.

In my cycle of defeat, I continued with the only thing that gave me false relief: denying my feelings, stuffing my emotions and medicating myself to relieve the pain that welled up inside me. It wasn't satisfying, but at the time, it was all I knew.

God, in all His glory, does not give up on us, even if we give up on ourselves. He also doesn't see us as we see ourselves. He opposes the proud, but welcomes the humble.

# Chapter
## Six
## *Radically Altered*

All those lost, sad and lonely years led to that definitive night in the bar in February, 2003. It really started out as most of my Friday nights did where I left work and headed to the nearest bar. I anticipated I would have a few drinks with my friends, laugh like I was all happy and temporarily forget all my mistakes, and the failure I'd become.

With the amount of alcohol I had ingested throughout the night, it was inevitable that my mouth would get me into trouble. I'd become a master over the years at suppressing all my feelings, though they continued to brew just out of sight. With the slightest excuse, such as too much alcohol, my emotions could easily rupture to the surface. The only thing that kept them at bay most of the time was an inherent desire to appear I was always in control. *What a lie!*

In my weakened state, the perfect storm transpired and I found myself irritated beyond belief at this woman. After our disparaging exchange of words, her fist may have just missed my face, but it hit the bull's eye of my shame and humiliation.

That was exactly what I needed to stop the insanity of my life and take a good, hard look inside. I knew it was time to stop running from the fear and pain. *God, how did I get here? Who did I think I was?* There was no more denying the fact that my life was spinning out of control and had been for many years. The events of that Friday night proved to me, without a doubt, that I was absolutely not in control of my self-destruction and if I didn't do something different, it would be the end of me. Despite my inconsistent, pitiful behavior, I desired to live a life with purpose. I wanted to belong somewhere and to someone. I needed to figure out how to fulfill those needs, quickly.

Sunday finally arrived and I awoke with a vigorous urgency and jumped in the shower, hoping to wash off at least some layers of humiliation from Friday night. No such luck. I was in great need of a drastic change and knew I needed to get to church as soon as I could. As fate would have it, it was Communion Sunday. God knows our needs even before we ask and had prepared this day for me many years ago.

As I walked into church, I worried others saw the humiliation written all over my face. Years of shame, guilt and condemnation seemed to ooze out of my pores and I couldn't hide it anymore. I don't remember the sermon that day, even though I sobbed through it, but I do remember the Communion. With my cup and bread in hand, I leaned over and rested my elbows on my knees. My mind recalled the events of the past few days, and other similar actions in my past and I wept. I silently cried out to God to wash me clean and forgive me for all my sins. I named them, one by one and asked for His forgiveness repeatedly. Never have I been more broken. I wondered if the people around me could hear the thoughts that thundered in my head. The tears continued until finally, after my plea for forgiveness over a lifetime of rebellion, immorality and disobedience, a calming peace washed over my heart and mind like a gentle tide sweeping over the sand. The tears finally subsided and with my eyes closed, I felt God's presence with me at that moment. I'd never repented with such sincerity before in my life and something felt different this time.

With a red nose and puffy eyes, I departed. The ride home was much lighter than the ride to church that morning. I went straight into my bedroom and fell to my knees in praise to the Lord who saved me from myself. I exclaimed to Him that I no longer could stand me and I wanted to change and be completely different.

"Make me brand new, God!" I exclaimed out loud.

No more running away from God; this time I ran to God. He'd waited for me for years. When I finally fell into His arms that day there was no condemnation for why it took so long, only an abundance of love. For the first time in my life, I wasn't afraid that God was mad or disappointed. His love for me was undeniable that morning. The heaviness was lifted off my chest for the first time since Friday night.

*I am finally free!*

It took numerous years of wandering in the desert for me to get to the end of myself and realize I could no longer live life on my terms and have any sense of peace. It simply was not possible. I needed a Savior to save me from my own destruction. Sin had taken me much further than I ever dreamed I would go and left a wake of death behind it. I was sick and tired of living that way.

When I got up off my knees that morning, I *was* a different person. My mind, heart and spirit had been transformed by God and I felt different. The first thing I wanted to do was apologize to my adversary from Friday night. With a new supply of grace, I called her cell phone and left a message and explained how sorry I was for what I'd said Friday night. Although quite intoxicated, that was no excuse for my behavior and I hoped one day she would find it in her heart to forgive me. When I hung up, another wave of peace came over me. *Hey, this obedience thing feels great!*

The second person I called was my dear friend, Jan Frisbie. I was enamored with her testimony of the miraculous transformation she'd experienced in her own life and I knew she could understand where I was at the moment. She and her dear husband, Frank, weaved in and out of my life several times during my rebellious years. Yet, all that time, she never judged me, she just fervently prayed for me. Finally, her prayer was answered.

"Jan! You're not going to believe what happened!" With excitement in my voice that was undeniable, I gave her the details from Friday evening's events through the morning's Communion and my subsequent surrender. I never thought I'd ever be happy from so much humiliation, but change can't infiltrate pride. My heart was changed and I knew it this time!

"Oh honey! I am so happy for you. I can hear the joy in your voice!" she exclaimed. Without hesitation, she knew I was different. Thus began a very tightly knit friendship with Jan and Frank Frisbie, who continue to this day to be beacons of light on my spiritual journey.

With absolutely no desire in my body to drink, I was finally free to explore the many options that God had for me and my life rotated in an entirely different direction. I had never existed without a constant need to suppress my emotions, so I wasn't quite sure what to do with myself. At Jan's suggestion, I dove into the Bible and began reading a chapter in Proverbs every day. It is a meaty book, full of wisdom and direction and it gave me insight into the kind of person I could be. When I read Proverbs 31, I realized I wanted to be the woman described in those beautiful scriptures. It seemed like such a long-shot, but I was determined to give it my best effort, if I ever married again.

All those years when Mom had instructed me to be self-reliant and not depend on a man, her intention was for my benefit, yet she spoke from a place of resentment in her own life. I was finally able to differentiate her intention from her anger, and realize how she was trying to encourage me. I was slowly becoming a confident, Godly woman, capable of taking care of myself, yet without resentment or bitterness. More than anything, I yearned to please God. As I grew closer to Him through His word and prayer, a hunger grew inside me that was unquenchable. I read the Bible with a new set of eyes and ears and my heart interpreted the words with revelation. I needed loads of wisdom and I found it within the pages of Proverbs.

When I made the decision to surrender my life February 23, 2003, my future was radically filled with hope. It no longer looked like a sad reflection of my past because God had a new adventure for me to explore with Him. Absent from Happy Hour, I had much more time on my hands. I eagerly began various DIY projects around my house to keep myself busy and give me a sense of accomplishment. Over the next few months, a dear friend, Juli, and I began the transformation of my home. Every room was painted a different color and I embraced the change. It went from boring white, to yellow, red, and even some leopard! The kitchen was the final room to paint and by that time, the creative juices were really flowing. Life seemed so much more colorful that I painted the kitchen lime green with red polkadots! In the morning when I walked into the kitchen, a smile stretched across my face. I called it the 'happy kitchen.' I now saw life through new lenses in full color, with great opportunities on the horizon.

When spring arrived, I dove into yard work and anything outside that needed my attention. I painted the trim on the outside of my house, hung shutters, and planted flowers. Juli was always willing to help, so we built a small fountain and pond in my back yard. With a new water fountain, my backyard became an oasis for me to relax and enjoy. There is something remarkably soothing about the sound of water washing over rocks. It was a word picture for me of how God's grace washed over my sins and continued to cleanse me.

As my external world took on a transformation, so did my heart. Fear no longer paralyzed me and I became willing to explore my past wounds with the help of spiritual mentors. I embraced the idea that if I worked through a wound, it could finally heal and became a scar that no longer dictated my actions. A scar represents an old wound that has healed and no longer causes pain. Open wounds, on the other hand, still have the ability to cause great pain if they are even touched and before, I had been a walking open wound. All those years of struggling to be a good person and yet failing miserably were because my open emotional wounds were hit again and again. They never healed and I was not willing to tend to them as needed. I was so afraid of what loomed in the recesses of my heart, that it was easier to ignore it. There was so much work to be done, but I reaped the benefits of more joy and freedom as I resolved issues from my past one at a time.

The most profound issue I had to face was about my parents. I'd suffered so many hurts from their volatile relationship when I was young, not to mention the pain of abandonment from their early deaths. No matter what problem I had in my life, ninety percent of all my dysfunction stemmed from my childhood in some respect. Sometimes, it was difficult to get to a place of resolution because I couldn't talk things out with my parents or say what needed to be said. In an effort to reach some closure, I wrote several letters to them to speak my mind and finally let the healing begin. It was hard sometimes to write what I needed to say, but I am grateful that I had wonderful support from friends who understood. Undergoing any kind of transformation is a process and when you are really struggling, it can be that support system of positive feedback that keeps things in perspective and allows you to move forward.

My little dachshund, Shorty was also a never ending source of unconditional love and the perfect companion. I'd had her since 1997 when she was only ten weeks old. For a woman who never had children, Shorty became my "dog child." Yes, I am one of those guilty pet owners who treats her dog like a baby. I have to say, Shorty is spoiled and undisciplined at times, but I love her unconditionally just as a parent would love their child. I've since had some much needed training from Cesar Milan, the Dog Whisperer.

Shorty was my friend, who eagerly greeted me at the door everyday with her unconditional love and excitement that warmed my heart the minute I laid eyes on her. If I'd had a bad day, her wagging tail and sloppy kiss could put a smile on my face instantly. There were some days I needed that desperately. Shorty's love for me portrayed an image as God loves me. Both God and Shorty offer unconditional love every day, no matter how bad I messed up yesterday or what mistakes I may have made. Neither remembers my past. For someone with a long history of mistakes, that kind of love is priceless.

Having Shorty also provided me with home security while living alone. At the slightest noise, she'd bark incessantly, eager to alert me of anything unusual. Having her next to me, I slept soundly every night with her protection. The companionship she's given me for the past fourteen years has truly been one of my greatest joys. As good a life as she's had, I pray she lives to be twenty-five, because it is not going to be pretty if that dog ever dies.

I also had human friends for support as well, and they have been pivotal in my life. Jan and I met years before, but became much closer after I surrendered my life. She shared the story of her life experiences before she made the decision to change and it was a life that resembled my past, but now had been transformed by Jesus. She'd allowed God to take her brokenness and use it to encourage others with similar backgrounds to enter into a relationship with Jesus and find peace. She was such a joyous person, full of love and compassion for everyone. I had always desired to have a life like hers someday. She and her precious husband, Frank, gently witnessed to me, not through words so much, but through their expressions of unconditional love. I watched them together and dreamed of having a marriage like theirs one day.

My two sisters, Tanya and Terri were great sources of support as well. Even though we all still struggled with our own burdens, I knew I could call them anytime with any problem. We leaned on each other, even if we weren't the sturdiest poles. We learned that through our hardships, we became much stronger than we could ever have imagined.

I also had two dear friends who made the transition with me and never left my side, Melissa and Robin. We were good friends prior to February 2003 and we enjoyed great times, but after my decision to change my life, they became even greater sources of support. They were there when I was at my worst and stuck close as I made the transition to a new life that looked nothing like the one I led when they first met me. They never missed a step. Melissa was never a partier, but saw me through that stage of my life and continued to support me no matter what. How difficult many nights must have been for her as I indulged in drinking and became my obnoxious, intoxicated self. Yet she never judged me or condemned me.

Robin and I were the rowdy, party girls of our threesome. We both were obnoxious when we drank and fed into each other that way, while Melissa sat quietly, watching us make fools of ourselves. After my transformation, I prayed fervently for Robin and before long, she too surrendered everything to Jesus and her life changed just as mine had. I can only imagine how elated Melissa must have been for both of us, (and herself as well).

Our relationships deepened when I made the decision to follow God—not because I became a better person, but because I became a more authentic person who was willing to be vulnerable. Any relationship has the opportunity to go much deeper when a person is willing to be authentic and open up their heart instead of hiding behind fear.

As God humbled me, my willingness to be my true self increased beyond my imagination. It's a shame that many people fear authenticity will lead them to rejection just as I did, when in most cases, it's just the opposite. The paralyzing lie had been exposed and I recognized it for the first time. It's frustrating being around someone who appears to have it all together while inside, you struggle with battles daily. When we're around someone like that, we are reminded that we *don't* have it all together, or so we believe. In my case, I perceived everyone to have it together and I was the only one who didn't. My fear was that somehow, they'd figure that out and leave me. Now, with a new set of lenses, I realize none of us have it together! Each of us has some insecurity about something. Even if it's just one thing. Instead of focusing on that insecurity, I decided to focus on something I could do well. Funny how it makes the magnitude of that insecurity shrivel back to its rightful size.

My life changed from anything I'd known before and I prayed God would lead me to meet more single women with whom I could fellowship and study the Bible. I could not get enough of Jesus and wanted to grow and learn as much as possible. While working as a sales representative in advertising, I met Cindy Freitag, (now Cindy Fisher). Within minutes our hearts connected beyond the usual small talk that began every sales call. I felt I'd known her for a long time. Her gentle demeanor was warm and trusting. She invited me to Bible Study at her house, along with her two roommates. I could not wait. God was so faithful to answer my prayer for Christian friends and that week, I attended a Bible Study at their house.

Pam, one of Cindy's roommates, was a joy to get to know, too. She had a heart bigger than Texas and would do anything for anybody, no question about it. Her demeanor was calm, gentle and quite unassuming. The first night I met her, I felt an instant connection, much like when I met Cindy.

Paula, Cindy's other roommate was a get-it-done type person. She spoke with authority and conviction every time her mouth opened. She'd been a faithful follower of Jesus for the past twenty-five years and was extremely knowledgeable about the Bible. Her desire was to lead us, and several others, including my dear friend, Tammy, into the power of living victoriously through a relationship with Jesus Christ. She taught us the power of the

Holy Spirit and the importance of a relationship with the Holy Spirit. This was all new information to me and like a sponge, I soaked up every ounce of wisdom from the Bible with each word spoken. The more I read God's Word, the more sense it made to me. Before, when I read the Bible, it seemed like a lot of do's and don'ts, but not anymore. I gleaned wisdom and instruction, but most of all, I learned how much God loved me. That is an example of the power of the Holy Spirit.

Cindy, Pam and Paula were exactly who I needed to meet at the right time. Being single and divorced was difficult for me because my life had changed exponentially and I needed new friends, new hang outs and new hobbies. Tammy and I worked together and became much closer as we studied the Word together. My circle of friends grew into God-fearing women who were divinely appointed to my life to help encourage me and strengthen my faith. While I had attempted Christianity in years past, now it was becoming very real to me.

Life rocked along smoothly for the next several months. I continued to go to Paula's Bible study and learned more and more about Jesus, His ways and His desire for my life. I also learned who I was in Christ and what that meant for my life. There were layers and layers of wrong beliefs, negative thoughts and judgments against myself that I had clung to over the years and it affected my self-image. As Paula heard me share some of these beliefs, she invited me to go through something called deliverance. I had never heard of deliverance and was somewhat fearful of what that was. Paula explained that deliverance was simply a severing of something (thoughts, beliefs, memories, negative behaviors passed down from my parents, bad relationships, and things of that nature) that kept me in bondage from doing God's will and living with freedom from my past. Once explained, I knew I absolutely wanted deliverance from all of the things she mentioned. I no longer wanted anything to be an obstacle to my freedom in Christ.

At Paula's suggestion, I started writing down anything that I currently struggled with or any emotions or behaviors from my past that might have been passed down from my parents. My list read something like this:

- Insecurities/low self-esteem/unworthiness/inadequate
- Selfishness/inconsistent behaviors
- Fear of abandonment/Fear of death
- Guilt, shame and condemnation for all my many mistakes and sins
- Alcohol abuse/myself in the past and my family members
- Immoral behaviors
- Anger/resentment/bitterness/unforgiveness
- Fear of success and fear of failure.

Just to name a few.

This was my first step to confronting the wounds and behaviors I'd tried to cover. Paula prayed out loud over me while laying her hands on my shoulders. As she prayed in the Spirit, God gave her more revelations about what I'd struggled with in my life. As Paula named them out loud, I felt a subtle release from guilt, shame and condemnation. Through Paula, God spoke to my heart and encouraged me to fully experience His love and to know He would never leave me nor forsake me - *ever*. He was with me during my childhood and saw everything that happened. He protected me during that time. He understood and forgave me for my sins of rebellion, immorality, and foolishness. I was encouraged to know God was never mad at me, but He does discipline His children for their own good and safety. God wanted good things for me, and did not allow bad things to happen out of some kind of punishment. That is not God's nature.

I realized during this process where many of the root causes for my beliefs and behaviors originated. When God gave me the revelation about the root of a particular behavior, it released me from the bondage of the underlying destructive belief. The destructive belief was always a precursor to the damaging behavior.

Through many salty tears and heartfelt prayers, my first deliverance was completed – the first of many. Imagine an onion with its thickest layer on the outside. That was the layer that was peeled off that day. A certain degree of freedom came from every layer being peeled away. Paula explained more issues would surface later, but that I couldn't handle them all at one time. It seemed we'd gone through so many with all the tears and prayers, but I found out later we'd barely scratched the surface.

Had I not been willing to go to those wounded places, I never would have heard the revelations, and subsequently received freedom from my past bondage. Had my heart continued to be prideful and protective, I never would have gleaned the positive effects of that prayer time. I was sick and tired of behaving the way I'd been for so many years. It never got me what I desired and I had nothing to lose by humbling my heart and receiving God's love, discipline and direction through the leadership of a mature, spiritual woman like Paula. My heart was ready and willing to continue to visit the wounds that kept causing my pain.

# Chapter
## Seven

*The Chains of Codependency*

Since those first small successes at uncovering the cause of many of my foolish behaviors, I've come to discover that the majority of my issues had to do with what the psychology world calls *codependency*. The term codependency originated in the field of alcoholism treatment. Alcoholics are dependent on alcohol. Family members are affected as well, so therapists began to call them *codependent*. I fondly refer to myself as The Queen of Codependency. Today people use the word to describe anyone affected by a relationship with a person who is manipulative, abusive, absent, or physically or mentally impaired.

Families are either functional or dysfunctional. In a functional family, the members learn to feel, trust and communicate openly without negative consequences. In turn, each member is considered a valuable individual and their value is not based upon their performance. Their significance and worth comes from who they are, not what they do.

However, in a dysfunctional family, mine included, the members do not learn how to feel, trust or communicate openly.

Often when they do try to communicate, consequences are negative and the communication turns into arguments. In my situation, I never witnessed my parents calmly resolve a conflict. My mom's alcoholism was a major factor that contributed to our dysfunctional family. Denial of feelings is common in people who come from this type of family because they are never encouraged to talk about them. Instead of having value because of who I was, I learned early on my value depended on my performance.

As a child, I felt if I stayed invisible and very quiet, no one would notice I was there and I therefore wouldn't be the cause of any problem. Children from dysfunctional homes rarely obtain a healthy identity and are at great risk for self-destructive behaviors and failed relationships. I should have tried out for the Codependency Poster Child.

Codependent people think others can only love them if they are perfect. Somewhere deep down they feel inherently bad. It's difficult, if not impossible, for a person who has come from a background like this to ever have a healthy relationship without some form of healing. I don't believe a healthy person would be able to exist very long in such an unhealthy situation.

In a dysfunctional family, there are several different roles the members take on as a way to cope. You might recognize yourself in one or many of these roles.

**Hero**

Sometimes this is the first-born child who often assumes responsibility that is not theirs. This child tends to take over the role of parenting the other children when one parent is extremely dysfunctional, for instance, when a mother is alcoholic. They become over-achievers academically or in sports, or in both arenas.

**Scapegoat**

Otherwise known as the "black sheep" of the family, this child acts out in negative ways to get any kind of attention. Because the focus in the family is on the dysfunction, the child seeks attention by running away, acting out at school, or making bad grades. More serious behaviors might include the abuse of alcohol or drugs at a very young age.

**Lost Child**

This child feels if they can stay quiet and inconspicuous then maybe the dysfunction will go away. They don't want to make waves or draw attention to themselves. They tend to fade into the background. This child tends to be timid, shy and extremely afraid.

**Mascot**

This is the child always trying to make light of the situation by being comical. The attempt at humor is the child trying to relieve all the tension in the dysfunctional home by telling jokes, acting silly and attempting to entertain. They want to make everyone else happy and if they don't succeed, that can become a frustration to them. Often they are not in touch with their own feelings on any level.

**Enabler**

This is the traditional role that would describe the relationship of one spouse to their alcoholic spouse. For instance, the wife of an alcoholic tries to keep her husband out of trouble and makes excuses for him. She might go so far as to call in sick for him when he's hung-over after an all night drinking spree. Rather than helping their spouse overcome, they are actually enabling their spouse to remain in their addiction.

These roles usually follow children into adulthood and often the dysfunction they experienced as a child is repeated in their own homes. It's also quite common for a child to take on characteristics of more than one role. For instance, I label myself as the Lost Child in my early years while living at home with my alcoholic mother, but then I took on characteristics of the Mascot, the Enabler and even the Hero, at different times of my life.

Sadly, these roles are what prevent a person from having a healthy relationship since chaos and drama are at the core. Growing up, chaos and drama was the norm in my home. It became my litmus test for what I thought was "normal."

Another important component to living a life of codependency is the extreme lack of boundaries. Good boundaries are imperative for a healthy relationship. Otherwise, the two people involved have no respect for each other. Growing up in a dysfunctional home, 'boundary' is a foreign word.

Many times a codependent person is controlling because, growing up, so much of their circumstances were out of control. They felt controlled by the symptoms of the dysfunctional family and never knew what to expect day to day. In short, by controlling as much as they can they are trying to protect themselves. Instead of gaining any real control over their lives, their behavior causes more issues and pushes people away.

At the core of the codependent's heart is the need and deep desire to be loved and gain approval. In their childhood dysfunctional home, that need was never met, so they go on a life long journey searching for someone who needs them or someone they could rescue to prove their worth. They don't want to be alone because they can hardly tolerate their own company. It's difficult for them to recognize the role they play in their many failed relationships because they tend to be victims. Rarely do they think they are the problem.

Many codependent people suffer from intense guilt and shame. Because of their need for other's constant approval, they always feel as if they are not good enough and don't measure up to expectations. They are in a constant dilemma to be good enough so someone will love them. However, codependents don't love themselves, therefore rendering it difficult to find someone else to love them. I was the perfect target for this type of dysfunction.

Many times codependent people will assume a false sense of responsibility towards others. They see through a different set of lenses that distorts everything negatively. If something goes wrong, they deem it must be their fault.

For a codependent person to heal, first and foremost, they must recognize that *their* behavior is not healthy. In my situation, I became depressed because of what I thought was a lack of approval of certain people. Because I could not get their approval, nothing else mattered. I became fixated on it and felt like a failure. This drove me to call a counselor so I could figure out how to have a better relationship with that person. When I mentioned my situation to my counselor, she said, very gently, she believed I suffered from codependency. I was shocked. Having been a psychology major in college, I knew all about codependency. However, I never dreamed I was the one suffering from it.

My counselor recommended a great workbook <u>Conquering Codependency: A Christ-Centered 12 Step Process</u> by Pat Springle, (www.mcgeepublishing.com). We discussed some of the questions in the workbook to determine the severity of my issue. Out of the fourteen questions, I answered "yes" to 12! Hence, my crown of Queen of Codependency! The good news was, I was ready to hear it. This was one more layer I was ready to peel back. I knew I needed to understand what was at the root of this issue.

Below is a list of the questions in *Conquering Codependency.* You may find yourself answering "yes" to many of these, or a few, or even part of a question. It was an eye-opener, I must admit.

1. Do I often feel isolated and afraid of people, especially authority figures?

___ Yes ___ No

2. Have I observed myself to be an approval-seeker? Do I lose my own identity in the process?

___ Yes ___ No

3. Do I feel overly frightened of angry people and of personal criticism?

___ Yes ___ No

4. Do I often feel I'm a victim in personal and career relationships?

___ Yes ___ No

5. Do I sometimes feel I have an overdeveloped sense of responsibility, which makes it easier to be more concerned with others than with myself?

___ Yes ___ No

6. Is it hard for me to look at my own faults and my own responsibility to myself?

___ Yes ___ No

7. Do I feel guilty when I stand up for myself instead of giving in to others?

___ Yes ___ No

8. Do I feel addicted to excitement?

___ Yes ___ No

9. Do I confuse love with pity, and do I tend to love people I can pity and rescue?

___ Yes ___ No

10. Is it difficult for me to feel or to express feelings, including feelings such as joy or happiness?

___ Yes ___ No

11. Do I judge myself harshly?

___ Yes ___ No.

12. Do I have a low sense of self-esteem?

___ Yes ___ No

13. Do I often feel abandoned in the course of my relationships?

___ Yes ___ No.

14. Do I tend to be a reactor instead of an actor?

___ Yes ___ No

A codependent person likely acquired the use of the above mentioned behaviors to cope with painful situations and never learned a healthy alternative. The various defense mechanisms listed below are how a codependent person learns to cope with painful situations. When I began the journey to emotional health, I realized these mechanisms were what I used to cope.

**People Pleaser**—This person is determined to make people happy and pleased at any cost. They usually completely lose their identity in all relationships. They shudder at the thought of anyone being disappointed or angry with them. The thought of someone's disapproval if they say "no" was too much for them to bear, so they always say "yes" even though they internally disagree.

**The Perfectionist**—The Perfectionist believes that if they do everything perfectly, then they would be acceptable and worthy. Because no one can be perfect, they are constantly disappointed and continually struggle with feelings of inadequacy.

**The Caretaker**—This is the person who takes care of others in an effort to avoid caring for themselves. They gain self-worth by taking on others responsibilities and needs.

**The Martyr**—A Martyr endures enormous pain and gets praise and self-worth for all they've withstood. The more praise they get, the more worthy they feel. They long for attention for the pain they endure. Sadly, no one asks them to endure the pain; they search for it for approval and praise. They feel pressured most of the time, yet the pressure comes from themselves.

**The Martha Complex**—This person believes they can work their way to gaining someone's approval. They believe that if they "do" enough, then they will be worthy. Yet, when others don't notice how much they've done, they're devastated and feel under appreciated. So, they do even more.

**The Stuffer**—They have never been allowed to express their feelings constructively, nor have they witnessed a role model expressing their feelings in a healthy way. The alternative is to stuff their feelings and internalize them. But a person can only stuff their feelings for so long and eventually, those feelings manifest in negative behaviors, or worse, explode one day like a volcano.

**The Fixer**—This person wants to fix everyone else's problems. One reason some engage in this behavior is because if they stay busy telling you how to live your life, they avoid dealing with their own issues. They may also feel significant if they can solve all your problems and therefore be worthy of your love.

When I read through the list, I checked yes to each one. I was off the charts with codependent behaviors!

As I mentioned earlier, controlling behaviors are a strong component of a codependent's nature. I realized after I answered a few questions about control that I suffered from it as well. Controlling people are usually the last to know. Do you feel you are ever controlling? Ask yourself the following questions:

- Do you feel someone in your family or circle of friends can't get by without your help?
- Are they are totally reliant upon you for something?
- Does it bother you or irritate you when other people are irresponsible?
- Do you find yourself taking on tasks that in reality, others should be doing?

There was no question about it; I was the Queen of Codependency. I walked the catwalk, received my crown and then got down to business. I swallowed my pride, got out of denial and realized the other people in my life didn't have the problem, it was actually me! I also realized that many of these behaviors were rooted in my very low self-esteem, poor self-concept and my grave lack of confidence. I was able to trace the negative behaviors all the way back to my childhood. This was not to place blame on anyone, but to realize where it all started and why. Going back to the root of the problem, not just addressing the symptoms was paramount in my healing process. As I understood why I developed those behaviors, I was able to forgive myself and move forward with the rest of my healing.

Recovery from codependency is about healing the wounds that keep you from having fulfilling relationships with others. It allows you to understand the emotions you attached to painful situations and move forward to a healthier behavior.

I've learned through the healing process, some of the more stubborn behaviors associated with codependency will rear their ugly head again and again. Old habits die hard. The difference is that now when I'm faced with that negative behavior, I am aware of it and stop to think about where it is coming from. I don't spend the next decade blaming someone else. Usually, within a day or two after prayer and self-examination, the answer comes to me. That is a huge aspect of becoming emotionally healthy; the willingness to look inside and to know that sometimes old behaviors will flare back up. Instead of spiraling into self-loathing, I can calmly ask myself, "Hmm? Where is that coming from?" God is so faithful to answer when I ask.

# Chapter Eight

## *From Broken to Blessed*

I have enjoyed the process of healing. For me, recovery from behaviors I struggled with for so long meant freedom and I didn't want anything holding me back anymore. What I've learned the most about codependency is how self-defeating it was to live as a victim all those years, trapped by my own negative behaviors. The bottom line was that I was responsible for my behaviors and distorted thinking and I was the only one who could change it. There is so much power in knowledge; never be afraid to learn more about yourself.

As I sought an intimate relationship with Jesus, I replaced my negative self-image with the image of who I was in Christ. I thought about myself as God would, as His child. As I allowed that type of unconditional love to wash over me, I loved myself in a healthy way. The brokenness ran deep in my heart and no other human could heal the hurts that swallowed me up. It took a Savior to repair the damage and make me new. He *never* saw me the way I saw myself.

From my brokenness and subsequent journey to healing, I have been able to empathize with others who have faced similar situations and used negative behaviors to deal with their pain. Once we free ourselves, we want others to experience that same freedom. I truly believe we are called to extend a hand to those with similar needs once we've healed and discovered the truth. The truth really does set us free!

Having gone through everything in my life from my childhood traumas, death of my parents, self-destructive behaviors and divorce, though it has been a long hard journey, it has all been worth it. I know I am a stronger person today having weathered those many storms. That's why I pray that through this book, you may be able to recognize any self-defeating behavior of your own that has held you back. While it may or may not be as extreme as my experience, any awareness and insight you can gain is worth it.

Layers kept peeling off of me and I continued learning how to implement boundaries in my own life. This applies to ALL relationships, whether it is with a boss, a sibling, a spouse or a child. Another great resource for this topic is a book titled *Boundaries: When to Say Yes, When to Say No, To Take Control of Your Life* by Henry Cloud and John Townsend. This book opened my eyes wide and revealed that I was allowing people to intrude much too far into many areas of my life because I had no boundaries. I actually believed that I didn't have the right to say "no" to many people; that their desires were more important than mine. This is such distorted thinking. I reasoned that if I said no, they would be upset with me but what really happened is that they lost respect for me.

Another realization I gleaned from the book *Boundaries* was this: if I say yes on the outside, but no on the inside, I am a liar! All of my life, I said yes on the outside and no on the inside. I was faced with the truth - I was indeed a liar! I now look at every request that way so when I am not able to say yes on the outside and yes on the inside, then the only thing I can honestly say, is no!

After reading that book, I began practicing saying no. When I say "practice" that's exactly what I mean. I said no a few times and sensed someone's disapproval then quickly went back to yes. But then I tried it again. And again. It won't come naturally if you've never had boundaries before. When you do and you remain committed, you will soon see that saying no will eventually become comfortable to you. In due time, you will discover that it's a healthy, responsible act to be true to yourself and much more important than gaining the approval of others. If you are guilty, like I was, of saying yes on the outside and no on the inside, you are definitely *not* being true to yourself or the other person.

One thing I learned about authenticity is if I can't be authentic with myself, I certainly cannot be authentic with anyone else. "Be true to yourself." How many times have you heard that phrase? What does that mean to you? For me, it means I have to be true to myself *first*, not because I'm selfish, not because I deserve more than anyone else, but because it determines the authenticity level of every relationship I enter.

It's been a long road to where I am today, and it isn't even close to over. Every day is a new opportunity to grow, learn, mature and experience joy on a higher level. I keep myself open to gaining more knowledge and apply what can help me grow even further. Dr. Phil once said, "You cannot change what you do not acknowledge." And to that I add: You cannot hide a changed heart!

The season I learned so much about myself was a difficult one, yet very liberating. Although divorced and living alone, except for Shorty, I was so in love with Jesus and the process of creating a new me. He was everything to me at that special time in my life. I had certainly become the Jesus Freak I'd been leery of in years past, but no longer cared because my heart was full of peace, finally. I was 100% sold out to living a life committed to learning; growing and becoming the person God wanted me to be.

I didn't feel I was denying myself the desire to be married again one day, but it was definitely a time of self-denial in an effort to heal my many battle wounds through God's love so that I might become the healthy wife I so desired to be.

As I drew near to Jesus, He certainly drew near to me. I spilled over with gratitude and yearned to serve Him – to give something back for all that He had done for me. It was not from a need to please or earn merit, but from an outpouring of love for Him.

In their book, *Why Good Things Happen to Good People*, authors Stephen Post and Jill Neimark state, "Celebration is, quite simply, the way we express gratitude. It's gratitude in action. Celebration moves us from fear to faith. Studies show that the most grateful individuals have often been through difficult and challenging experiences. Individuals who have overcome adversity in youth are more optimistic and grateful than the average person. It can also inspire us to profound giving-such as donating organs to save the lives of strangers-according to a new study out from IRUL" (The Institute for Research on Unlimited Love).

One night I prayed for God to give me an opportunity that I could give back; some way I could be of use to Him out of my overflow of gratitude. I deeply desired to do something 'big' for Him. Little did I know what God had planned was beyond my wildest dreams. All His goodness was a welcomed surprise because I'd never experienced God that way.

# Chapter
## Nine

## *We Can't Out Give God*

I can't recall the first time I heard the phrase, "It's better to give than to receive," but I know what I thought every time I heard it: *how can it be better to give than to receive?* As a child, it was easy to receive presents. Someone gave me a gift and I tore into the packaging as quickly as I could. As a child, the more I could get, the better I felt, or so the lie goes.

My selfish nature died on February 23, 2003, and a new nature formed inside me. It was then that I learned the truth about it being better to give than to receive. Jesus gave me a new lease on life and a chance to live life abundantly. My heart desired to give that away to others, and especially to give back to God. Interestingly, God never asks us to give Him anything; He only asks us to believe and receive His free gift of salvation. Yet, with a heart so full of gratitude, it's difficult not to want to give back.

There's an enormous difference between giving out of expectation and giving to bless. The first comes from our selfish nature; the latter comes from Godly inspiration. I asked God for divine appointments during my prayer time. A divine appointment was an opportunity put in my path to bless someone else by sharing the message of hope with them. I wanted them to know how God changed my heart, and how much He loved them. At the end of the day, I enjoyed remembering the divine appointment in my path. I knew I was at the right place at the right time. Quite different from being at the wrong place at the wrong time. A great sense of purpose came from knowing that. For someone who'd lived most of her life in shame and condemnation, I can't tell you what a difference it made to know God's will that day for my life.

There are endless ways to give and serve. One of the simplest ways is to smile and acknowledge someone, although, I'm quite let down if I smile at someone and they don't smile back. I never understood that. A genuine smile and greeting can have a positive effect on someone, especially someone who feels down, lonely, or invisible. Of course, the more obvious forms include giving tangible items to those in need, money to the church to further God's missions or donating your time. I've only mentioned a few, but the ways to give and serve are limitless. The beauty of giving and serving is that God will reveal to you areas that best fit your gifts and talents.

You may be hesitant to offer yourself out of fear that God would send you to a far away land as a missionary and to be honest I can relate to that. A few times, I caught myself praying, "Lord, I want to serve You, just not in Africa, please." However, one of the most amazing opportunities I've experienced was on a mission trip to Managua, Nicaragua. There, a group of us served children who literally lived in a dump ground. The missionaries of Savior's Tear Ministry, (www.saviorstear.org) built a school for those children to get them out of the dump ground. Their mission gives the children a Christian education, two meals a day and love and encouragement to become the person God always intended for them to be. For five days, our team set up camp at their school and loved on them, taught them new games and sports, and worshiped with them.

Those children had nothing, yet they were the happiest people I'd ever laid my eyes upon. I couldn't understand how they could be so carefree, and God answered my question. In my spirit, I felt God say, "Dawn, these people are so happy because they don't know to want anything more. They aren't bombarded with commercials and advertising that tempts them. Their daily needs are met and that is enough for them." Wow! What a convincing response from God. I think about that often as I lose my patience, or wish I had a new 'something.'

I was so sad to leave those precious children because I'd grown close to them, their pure hearts and the love in their eyes. As a team, we worked hard to serve them, but in the end, we were the ones who walked away blessed and changed. To see their happiness from us giving them love and affection was the most treasured gift I could have ever received.

Give freely with no expectations. Our expectations limit God and His ability to bless us. When you give from the fullness of your heart, God blesses you from the fullness of His heart. And let me tell you, He has an extremely full heart.

Another answer to my desire to give back to God in a big way came in September, 2004. I remember the day like it was yesterday. My cell phone rang and on the other end was my dear friend, Jan. We visited for a moment then she asked me to keep Norm Saunders, a man I had briefly met the previous year while participating in our church's Christmas Pageant, in my prayers. Norm needed to go back on the kidney transplant list because they didn't think he could take much more dialysis. My heart sank when I heard that news.

I didn't know Norm had kidney problems and was horrified to learn he'd already had one kidney transplant a few years prior. Norm's own kidneys slowly stopped functioning after years of undetected high blood pressure. All this kidney information was foreign to me. I didn't know anyone who'd had a kidney transplant or even difficulties with their kidneys. In fact, the information I had was limited and inaccurate. I assumed only a family member could donate a kidney. I blurted out to Jan, "What about his family; could they give him a kidney?" Jan explained they had been tested, but weren't good matches for Norm. My heart sank even further. I felt helpless and sad by Norm's situation. Yet, I burst out with: "Could I donate my kidney to Norm?" Jan was surprised by my question and frankly, so was I. *Where on Earth did that come from?*

She said the first thing I should do is have a blood type test done because the donor and recipient needed to have similar blood types. Jan knew that Norm's blood type was A negative. According to the American Red Cross, only 7% of U.S. caucasians have A negative blood type (www.redcrossblood.org). I decided to take the test that evening after work and let her know immediately. I was almost certain my blood type was A positive. Within a few minutes, the conversation went from praying for Norm to offering to donate my kidney. *How in the world did that happen? Lord, is this the answer to my prayer?*

The emotion I felt the remainder of the day was one of delightful anticipation. I prayed out loud to God with cautious enthusiasm. "Lord, I want to help Norm if I possibly can. If this is Your will, God, please let us be a match; if not, then don't let us match at all."

I felt complete peace about offering to give Norm my kidney which was amazing in itself. This was so out of character for me. I was so afraid of pain; any kind of pain. I couldn't even be in the same room while Shorty got a shot or her nails clipped! (No wonder I never birthed any children; I might have died from the pain!) I knew this had to be from God.

That evening, I went after work to get my blood tested. I thought the excitement flowing through my veins would certainly be detected by the technician. I wanted nothing more than to be able to help Norm live another twenty-five healthy years with his family.

Terrified of needles, I imagined myself lying on a beautiful white sandy beach with the sun beaming down on my skin, warming me as the ocean misted in the air. My blood slowly filled the vile and I became queasy. The technician finally pulled the needle out of my arm and I realized I'd made it and didn't pass out.

I waited but I didn't worry. I knew I had done all I could and the rest was up to God. The technician returned within a few minutes and declared my blood type was A negative! "Are you sure? I thought I was A positive?" I questioned.

She smiled and said, "Yes, Ma'am, I've been doing this a long time and I am positive that your blood type is A negative." (I guess she put me in my place).

I drove to the Church parking lot where I knew I'd find Jan's van as she and Frank were at choir practice. With sheer elation, I wrote on the back of my business card, "I'm A negative!" I left it on her windshield. I was so excited that we were a match and believed this was from God. The very fact that I could possibly be used by God was the best thing to ever happen to me.

Jan called me after choir practice and the joy in her voice was like music to my ears. She couldn't believe Norm and I were the exact same blood type. She arranged for Norm and I to meet the following day. I could hardly sleep that night before our meeting. The next morning, I met Norm and his precious wife, Karen. When our eyes met, I saw a spark of hope. He was amazed that a stranger would donate a kidney to him. (I was amazed at how tall he was). Little did he know the prayer I'd prayed just a few months earlier. After everything Jesus did for me, I was beyond thrilled to do something for Him. Despite my disdain for needles and a very low threshold for pain, I had no fear of an operation. I was determined to offer my kidney to Norm. That seemed the least I could do after everything Jesus had done for me.

After pleasantries, Norm asked if I was certain about donating my kidney. With bold confidence I said, "Absolutely! I have complete peace about this!" That simple statement began a journey of love, sacrifice and unbelievable joy.

Overnight, Norm and Karen escorted me into the inner circle of their family. Without a doubt, I finally felt like I belonged somewhere and with someone; it was the best feeling I'd had in many years. Within days, I met Norm and Karen's daughter, Kendra and son, Kyle, his wife, Leesa and their families. Kendra's daughters, Railey and Kellyn, latched onto me and I to them. It seemed like a fairy tale to have this family take me in as one of their own. The atmosphere was one of celebration and joy and I was so thankful to be a part of such a loving family. Their family was so different than anything I'd ever experienced. They genuinely enjoyed one another's company and their love was obvious. They showed me what a real family could be. My cup spilled over with blessings.

In a matter of six short weeks, all the testing was completed and the surgery was scheduled for October 26, 2004. That was a miracle all in itself as the doctors told us the testing process usually took several months, not weeks. Despite this being Norm's second transplant, his insurance covered both our surgeries! No doubt, another miracle for the books. Since my left kidney was easiest to harvest, we decided to name it Lucy.

The Sunday before the surgery, Pastor Jonathan Mast gave a message of how one life can make a difference between despair and hope. At the end of the service, Jan, Norm and I went down and the congregation prayed for us and the upcoming surgery. As the congregation witnessed our love for one another, they were brought to their feet as God continued to work miracles throughout this event. In that moment of intense love, the congregation engulfed us with God's perfect assurance. They stood with us throughout our journey with their prayers, love, support and faith.

The next morning, the newly named "Caravan of Hope" met at my house. Norm, Karen, and Kendra in one vehicle; and Jan, Frank and myself in another. Sweet Jan agreed to stay with me because she couldn't bear the thought of me being in the hospital room by myself. That was a huge sacrifice for Jan. She and Frank had rarely been apart from each other. I cannot express how grateful I was to her for being there with me throughout the entire procedure. I will never forget her kindness toward me.

We checked into a hotel near the hospital and deposited our luggage. Later on, a few minutes before midnight, we loaded up in the caravan and went a few blocks to the hospital. Following medical instructions, I was weak from no food and an empty digestive system, but my attitude was one of joy and celebration. It didn't feel like Norm and I were about to have a surgery, it felt like we were about to celebrate a birthday. The surgery was scheduled for 7:00 a.m., so the nurses put us in a room across the hall from each other. The atmosphere was more like a college dormitory than a hospital. We flitted to each other's room, visiting, giggling and praying for the surgery's success. I did not have one fear at all; just pure joy and celebration. Around 2:00 a.m., we went to our respective rooms and slept for a few short hours before the nurses came for us.

The early morning came quickly and before long, I was transferred to a gurney and an intravenous preparation for anesthesia was given. Counting backward from one hundred, I fell into a deep slumber for the next five hours. Our friends and family were told the surgery to harvest the kidney would take about two hours, so when that time came and went, those waiting for us became anxious. The first memory I have after waking from the surgery was lying in my hospital bed, sluggish from the anesthesia and *starving*. The first food I requested was fried cheese. Jan, in all her loving kindness, didn't have the heart to tell me that dinner would consist of ice chips. She diverted my requests for a while longer. I thought for certain when I woke up, I would get a meal of my choice, but my body could not have handled it.

Shortly after I arrived in my room, Norm was taken to his. The report was that Lucy, Norm's new kidney, began functioning in the operating room before they closed Norm's abdomen. Jan visited Norm and noticed he was pink in color. Lucy began filtering impurities from his body and it showed. He laughed and talked telling everyone he had his own personal 'angel.' Truly, a celebration like none other took place that day in October.

The next several days consisted of a slow but steady recovery. Jan and I walked the hallways back and forth to Norm's room, as directed by my doctor. The more I moved around, the sooner I would be discharged. Norm and I became the talk of the nursing staff on the renal floor. They were inspired by our story and love for one another and could hardly believe that just six weeks prior, we were strangers. It certainly didn't show in our behavior. Norm continued to recover and his new kidney performed flawlessly. The celebration continued.

Six days after the transplant, my discharge arrived. I was saddened to leave Norm and Karen at the hospital, but Jan and I wanted our own beds like none other. Norm had to stay another week for his kidney function to be monitored before his release. Jan was the best roommate I could have asked for. Not only did her nursing background come in extremely handy, her precious love for me and the Lord filled my room with peace. Having her by my side was undeniably a gift from God. All in all, it was not a difficult surgery and I would do it again if I had another kidney to give away.

Norm and I recovered from our surgeries and began rehearsals for the Christmas Pageant in November. He would again be the Big Red King and I continued to play an angel in the production. Norm and I both tired easily during rehearsals, but managed to make it through all of them and all six productions. It was heavenly. Every time I saw Norm's six foot seven stature walk down the aisle toward the stage, tears welled up in my eyes. He looked at me and gave me a quick smile and my heart jumped for joy. I was so thankful for the friendship and love that supernaturally occurred between him, his family and myself. It was simply indescribable.

That year, the Thanksgiving and Christmas holidays were spent with Norm and his family and I felt I belonged there with them. Being with them was so natural and comfortable. They insisted I be in their Christmas card, too. I'd never seen such love and joy between so many people in one family. It gave me hope that I could one day have a family as wonderful as Karen and Norm's.

The community was also so supportive of Norm and me and many people couldn't believe I'd given a stranger a kidney. I never understood what was so hard to believe. I mean that with all sincerity. In my honest opinion, having and raising children is many times more difficult and sacrificial than giving a kidney to anyone, even a stranger. I have, however, often wondered why we have two well-functioning kidneys. I asked both surgeons and neither of them with all their "kidney" education and background could give me a reason why the body has two kidneys when it only needs one to function. Could it be that God made us with two just so we could give one away? I certainly believe that now.

During my experience, I became quite interested in the transplant process. After visiting one of the kidney dialysis centers, my heart was broken for all those who sat in their recliners to undergo the four hour process of cleansing their blood. Many patients have someone who is willing to give their kidney, but for medical reasons and incompatibilities, they are unable to donate to their loved one.

As I researched the topic, I came across an organization that matches an incompatible donor and recipient with another donor/recipient pair who also are not a match, The Alliance for Paired Donation (APD.) Their website is www.paireddonation.org. The donor of the first pair gives to the recipient of the second pair and vice versa. They basically swap kidneys. This program has also introduced a new way of accepting non-simultaneous donations which is helpful because the transplants no longer have to be performed at the same time.

For the 88,000 plus people in America who are waiting for a kidney transplant, that has to be great news. However, about twelve of those patients will die every day because there aren't enough donors.

To date, one of the greatest blessings in my life was the opportunity to give Norm a kidney. I have never encountered any kind of medical issue due to donating my kidney and subsequently, living with only one. In fact, I sometimes forget I have only one kidney because my body performs exactly as it did before the surgery, actually, a little too efficient at times. I hope that any fear associated with organ donation would dissipate through education and that more people will offer their organs, even for a stranger.

# Chapter
## Ten

## *Husband Checklist: 101*

As winter turned to spring I developed a little spring fever. Spring is my favorite time of year. It symbolized new life, hope and a refreshing perspective that replaced winter's short, cold days. My winter was spent enjoying the family of Norm and Karen and how well they functioned as a family unit. I'd now seen two healthy marriages in Jan and Frank, and Norm and Karen. For the first time in my life, I witnessed what a healthy family resembled. The desire to live the rest of my life with a loving husband in a healthy marriage bubbled up inside me.

Three years had passed since my divorce and I wondered if the happily ever after dream that I held in my heart might come true one day. I was grateful beyond measure for all the loving people God placed in my life, and of course, for Shorty, but it seemed I lacked something - that special someone. I placed the responsibility of a husband in God's hands and waited for Him to deliver.

I went from being single until I was thirty, to married for six years, and back to single for another three and a half years. It was during those three and a half years that I learned to live content with my own company. Many nights I cooked spaghetti for myself and called it my "romantic dinner for one." I never dreamed I'd actually enjoy my own company.

Jesus is the best husband to a single woman and He never disappoints. One day, I went to a jewelry store and bought a ring I wore on my left hand ring finger. I decided that while I was single with no Earthly mate, I considered myself 'married' to Jesus. I proudly wore that ring like an engagement ring with a three carat diamond!

I needed to work on myself and many issues, and I couldn't do that effectively if there had been another person around that I was focused on. As a single woman during this time, my two main concerns were Jesus and Shorty. My time was focused on issues that concerned Jesus and His will for me. It truly was a precious season.

As I slowly transformed into the woman God intended, I believed I could also someday be the wife He intended. As much as I enjoyed my sweet time with Jesus, deep down, I desired to spend my life with an earthly husband. God knew that, too. He's the one who gave me that desire in the first place so I'm sure it didn't come as a surprise to Him.

Eager to learn God's design for marriage, I listened to an audio CD series by Jimmy Evans, Pastor of Trinity Fellowship Church in Amarillo, Texas. The series was entitled *Our Secret Paradise* and was a teaching resource to encourage married couples. Although still single, the teaching gave me such hope. The statement I'll never forget from that series was this: "We're all messed up!" You might wonder how a statement such as that could give me hope, but it did.

My entire idea of marriage was a misconception based on a fantasy. Before, I dreamed marriage would be the perfect union between two perfect people. I was so determined to have the opposite kind of marriage my parents had in the past, yet I had no tools or knowledge on how to accomplish that. So what did I do? I did exactly what they did. In my previous relationships, perfectionism reared its ugly head and where there is perfectionism, disappointment always follows. Divorce was imminent.

I actually thought that if I was perfect, then I would have a perfect marriage. *How unrealistic and warped is that thinking?* I can never be perfect, my spouse can't be perfect and because of that, neither could our marriage. No one is perfect. Pastor Jimmy stated that in marriage, two messed-up people join together and they each bring their emotional baggage and wounds from their past. In a healthy, *not perfect*, marriage, those two people have an opportunity to become each other's redeemers. We all have a choice in marriage: we can either hurt our spouse, or help heal our spouse.

The knowledge I gleaned from that message was to not set out to be the perfect wife - I would fail at every attempt and leave myself disappointed. I also no longer searched for the perfect husband - he was a figment of my imagination. My dream of a perfect marriage died too. However, I replaced my dream of a perfect marriage with one of a healthy marriage. I now desired a marriage that encouraged and fostered healing - where the two of us had no desire to hurt each other and would sacrifice for one another graciously. Once unbound from my idea of a perfect marriage, I allowed myself permission to be who I really was, *all messed up*. I would also allow my spouse to be who he really was, *all messed up, too!*

It was about this time that I had a brush with my past. Just as we make a breakthrough and are traveling along a new path at a brisk pace, our old tendencies and fears can rear their ugly heads. One night, I decided to go to dinner with some friends from my past. I hadn't seen some of the girls for a while and they asked what I did now with my time, since I didn't go out anymore.

"Well, I hang out with Norm and Karen, go to church and go to Bible study. That's about it." My answer seemed quite simple, even to me. You could have heard a pin drop. By their lack of comment, I discerned my answer might have made them uncomfortable. I know I certainly felt uncomfortable after I said it. All of a sudden, I was on a different planet than they were and I looked like an alien to them. That old feeling of 'not belonging' sprung a leak inside me.

When I arrived home I broke down in tears. The obvious discomfort at dinner with my answer caused me to feel judged and disapproved of just like I used to. Out of nowhere came old emotions that were linked to pleasing others and needing their approval. I questioned where I was in life and a sense of loneliness overcame me like a tidal wave. How I perceived the girl's reactions to my new lifestyle may or may not have been correct, but that particular night, it pierced my heart. I sensed that, from their perspective, I lived a dull life. But I knew my life was anything but boring. I'd learned to deal with life head-on in a healthy manner. Yet, why did I feel so out of place all of a sudden? The feelings that overcame me the next few days were hard to understand and I felt depressed the more I thought about it. A heaviness and grief came over me that I couldn't shake.

I decided to seek professional counseling and I'm grateful I did. The first two sessions uncovered the source of grief. I had finally let go of the guilt from my divorce, yet the shame remained. Fossum and Mason say in their book, *Facing Shame*, that "While guilt is a painful feeling of regret and responsibility for one's actions, shame is a painful feeling about oneself as a person." I punished myself without mercy and was incapable of forgiving myself.

My counselor asked if I had stayed married, would I have given Norm the kidney? After a moment of thought, I answered with an emphatic, "No." For one thing, if I was still married, I didn't believe the opportunity to give my kidney to Norm would have ever presented itself. Although I was quite aware of how God felt about divorce, He was also able to turn something bad into something good. After contemplating my life without the blessing of Norm and his family, I realized, God was giving me good gifts. He wasn't punishing me, I was still punishing myself, over and over. Finally, a release of the shame of my failed marriage ensued. It felt good to be absolved of it and let it go for the first time.

My third and last visit with my counselor was about moving past the divorce and stepping into the future God had in store for me. I was eager to do that. She recommended I complete two writing exercises. First, write down how my life would look if I remained single and never married. Could I be happy with that scenario? Second, write down a list of characteristics I desired in a spouse. I could put anything on the list I wanted.

That evening, which was Friday, April 22nd, Norm's granddaughters spent the night with me. We had the best time painting crafts on my kitchen table and talking about their issues with their friends at school. It amazed me that these two girls trusted me so much and enjoyed spending time with me. Most of my life, I felt untrustworthy, but I realized that God had changed my heart. I *was* a new person and I *was* trustworthy now. When I considered where I was emotionally at their age, it astounded me to hear them speak with such spiritual maturity. It made my heart jump with joy because I knew Jesus lived in them and they had great futures ahead. We all four snuggled that night in my queen sized bed: Railey, Kellyn, Shorty and me. It was truly one slumber party I'll never forget.

The next morning, Norm and Karen came by and we all went to eat breakfast. My fortieth birthday was three days away, so Norm and Karen brought my present to me. A tree! A real live tree! They wanted to give me a 'forever' gift. Within minutes, Kyle in his brute strength had a hole dug and the tree planted in my backyard. I loved that gift more than I could express. Their thoughtfulness overwhelmed my heart with joy. The little girl inside me wanted that feeling to last forever.

That evening, Norm, Karen, and their entire family took me to dinner for my birthday. It was an extraordinary celebration and I didn't want the evening to end. The warmth I felt from them was magical, safely and securely wrapped in their love and acceptance.

When I returned home that evening, I realized that my life would be just fine if I stayed single. That, of course, wasn't my first choice, but I knew, without a doubt, I was loved and that's all I'd ever longed for.

I had Jesus, great friends to fellowship with, my two older sisters and family who loved me, and of course, Shorty, just to mention a few wonderful aspects of my life. But deep down, I still hoped that one day I would be someone's wife.

Then I began work on the second assignment. One thing I knew for certain, I would only allow God to choose my spouse. I believed that if I allowed God to choose my mate, the relationship would be peaceful and right. There would be no breaking-up and getting-back-together behavior. I believed the two of us would know if we were right for each other, and there would be no guesswork or fear.

My list was specific as to my deepest desires. Below is the list I wrote that night:

Qualities that are a must:

1) He loves the Lord (already), meaning he already has a relationship with the Lord and he is committed to growing that relationship. He reads the Bible, attends church and prays on his own.

2) I'm attracted to him - there is chemistry between us.

3) He's funny, quick-witted and loves to laugh.

4) He's not too serious, and not a workaholic.

5) He's adventurous, but not a show-boat kind of guy.

6) He sees me and pursues me.

7) He's a leader in life and in this relationship, confident.

8) He's secure, but not arrogant. He's not a jealous type, but can show concern and affection.

9) He CAN communicate!

Additional qualities I hope he has:

10) Likes to do projects around the house with me.

11) Can and likes to two-step/jitterbug/country dance.

12) Is not a drinker/smoker. (I don't really care if he drank a beer, but does he **have** to?)

13) Enjoys hanging out with my friends.

14) Enjoys going out to eat at fine dining restaurants; eating desserts, going to the theater, riding rides, dressing up for events.

15) Loves Shorty - almost as much as me.

16) Can relax and sit still sometimes.

17) Enjoys NASCAR

18) Enjoys working out, but is not obsessive about it.

19) Would be willing, (as a married couple someday) to teach Bible study.

20) People know and respect him. He doesn't have a bad reputation that precedes him (recently); and they say, "Oh, what a nice guy-what a good guy."

21) Has a respectable job and is respected at his job.

After I finished writing the list, I read over it and decided it represented my desires well. I believed God knew the desires of my heart already, but it was important for me to write them down. I'd never been in a healthy relationship and I needed a road map to that unknown destination. Just as with any goal, it becomes more concrete after it's written down.

For those of you who are already married and wished you would have written a list first, I encourage you to write a list now, and include all the aspects of your spouse that you were attracted to when you dated. Sometimes, we easily forget the wonderful, endearing qualities of our spouse after years of marriage. This can be a gentle reminder of why you fell in love.

There are many worse things that can happen to a person besides being single. For example, I believe it is much worse to be married and lonely, than single and alone.

If you are still single now, yet deeply desire to be married, I encourage you to write out the two assignments that were given to me and place it in the care of God. He knows the desires of your heart. In Psalms 37:4, the Scripture states, "Delight yourself also in the LORD, and He shall give you the desires of your heart" (NKJV).

I didn't want to go into another marriage with completely unrealistic expectations. God's intent for marriage is that we heal each other. My parents clearly hurt each other in their marriage, and I hurt my spouse in my previous marriage. I knew after living through the devastation of a divorce, I wanted to marry the right person, at the right time and leave nothing to chance. I never wanted to go through divorce again. God renewed my mind by healing wounds from my past and gave me hope for such a marriage. I held a fervent anticipation that one day, I, too, would be happily married.

The map was drawn and I knew what I desired in a spouse. The petition was made to God and the rest was in His hands. Satisfied, I drifted off to a peaceful sleep that night.

**\*\*\*\***

The prestigious Kidney Foundation Golf Tournament never crossed my radar until I met Norm and donated my kidney. I'd learned ample amounts of information regarding kidney donation and about our local kidney foundation organization. Every year, they held an annual fundraising golf tournament to benefit the area's patient care expenses, such as transportation to and from the dialysis center, monies to help pay for exorbitant costs of medication and other expenses. After the donation, I was asked to be on the Board of Directors of our local foundation to bring a donor's perspective. Eager to share my experience about donation, I jumped on board.

One unseasonably cold April day, Karen and I volunteered at the Kidney Foundation Golf Tournament and registered players as they arrived. Once everyone was checked-in, they proceeded to their assigned hole and the tournament began. Norm, being the avid golfer he was, competed in the golf tournament that day and Karen and I looked forward to driving the cart around to watch him play. However, after a few minutes, a team called into the clubhouse and stated they didn't have an official scorekeeper. The winner of the golf tournament would be awarded a round at the prestigious Pebble Beach golf course, so every team had to have an official scorekeeper. Karen and I were asked to score the team, which was the Happy State Bank team. We didn't have any pressing duties, so we obliged and headed to the fifteenth green where they were. Upon arriving, each team member came over and introduced himself: Dave Hutson, Kerry Adair, Keith Bjork and Gary Wells. I'd just heard Gary's name the week before when a friend of mine, Bill Bandy, asked me to attend a local fundraising banquet and sit at his table, along with his parents, another couple, whom I knew, and *Gary Wells*. I asked Bill if Gary was the guy who'd lost his wife to cancer the year before and Bill said, "Yes, he was." Nothing else was said about Gary, and I declined to go to the banquet, subsequently missing the opportunity to meet him that night.

Yet, right before my eyes, stood that same Gary Wells. I thought to myself, "Well, I guess I was supposed to meet him after all." I remember his bright blue eyes from the first few seconds of our meeting. His smile was warm and genuine. With his distinguished gray hair, he fit the banker mold to perfection. Despite the cold, wet weather, I looked forward to following his team around all day to keep their score. Karen and I wondered about Gary; what kind of guy he was, and if he was a Christian. She and I began making assumptions based on his every move and word spoken. First of all, he was a great golfer. Golfing was not on my list of characteristics required, but it was nice to know he was good at it. If he hit a bad shot, he certainly didn't seem too upset or take himself too seriously. That was a definite plus.

At one time, Gary jumped into our cart to get out of the rain while waiting his turn. My heart skipped a beat when he slid in next to me, but I remained calm with a smile wider than the Grand Canyon across my face. I remarked, "Well, at least the wind isn't blowing."

Gary chimed in with, "Thank You, Lord!" Karen and I caught eyes and smiled thinking the exact same thing: *He must be a Christian after saying that!* Not much of a test for faith, but we were certain he followed Jesus after making a statement like that.

Throughout the day, the temperature continued to drop and I thought I was going to freeze. If there was any negative side effect after the surgery it was this: my tolerance for cold weather dropped to zilch! The guys were kind enough to loan me their extra rain gear and gloves which helped me stay warm. I was most grateful since I certainly didn't come prepared for such a cold, wet day.

We followed them all day long and celebrated great shots and mourned the bad ones. Toward the end of the day, Gary sank a forty-foot putt and we all jumped up and down in celebration of his great shot! Everyone gave each other high-fives and when Gary approached me, we slapped a high-five, and he said, "That shot deserves a hug!" I was surprised by his statement, but delighted to give him a hug. My heart jumped a few beats faster.

Karen and I had plenty to discuss upon returning to our golf cart while we followed them to the next hole. We read much more into that hug than what it represented, but it was fun to dream. Karen really liked Gary and I did too. Even though I'd only known him a few hours, I was convinced he was a great guy. I also knew that he lost his wife after a long battle with breast cancer. She was only forty years old when she died. I'd heard wonderful things about his late wife and her faith as she battled the disease. Having lost my mom to breast cancer when she was fifty-one years old, I considered that to be one topic we shared on some level.

When the team finally hit their last shot, we hurried to the clubhouse for warmth and food. Gary and I found ourselves visiting with each other while everyone else checked to see if they'd won the golf tournament. Through our brief dialogue, we discovered our hometowns were only seventeen miles apart. What a small world!

I needed to remove the rain gear the guys had so graciously loaned me throughout the day, so I put my hand on Gary's shoulder to balance myself as I pulled my rain pants off. That was quite a bold move on my part and I even surprised myself when I did it. What happened next confounded me even more. The minute I was back on my two feet, Gary said he had to go and it was nice meeting me and he vanished. I couldn't believe it. Disappointed that he left so quickly I wondered if I'd been too brazen by putting my hand on his shoulder to balance myself. Without delay, I found Karen and explained what just took place. In Karen's usual calm, faithful manner, she assured me I hadn't offended him. That night, I fell into my warm bed without a better understanding of why Gary disappeared, but it didn't matter anymore. I'd had such a wonderful day and was filled with a new hope. Even if I never saw Gary again, I was grateful for the gift of spending the day with him at the golf tournament. If nothing else, I learned there are guys out there and available who love God, and are a lot of fun. I couldn't stop smiling. My heart was swollen with thankfulness. I had my electric blanket and Shorty by my side - all was well. The next day was my fortieth birthday and I was eager to see what blessings and opportunities God had for me.

# Chapter
## Eleven

### *He Had Me at "Dachshund"*

Birthdays are one of my favorite days of the entire year. Since my birthday falls toward the end of the month on the twenty-sixth, I begin the celebration the first day of April. I like to call it 'Birthday Month.' But nothing surpasses the specialness of the actual birth *day*. Meeting Gary the day before was one of the best birthday gifts I've ever had. I couldn't stop thinking about him and I couldn't stop smiling. Since he didn't ask for my number before he darted off, I wondered if I'd ever see him again, but tried not to dwell on that too much. I had so much to be thankful for with my family and friends nearby and a new hope in my heart.

I visited with Karen and expressed my desire to see Gary again, and she suggested I take him the photos of his team she took the day of the golf tournament. Gary did mention to me that he worked at the bank branch on Soncy Road and to come by anytime and he'd give me a tour. *Should I be so bold? Why not?* Nothing ventured, nothing gained. The tournament was on Monday and Friday had rolled around. Karen gave me the photos and encouraged me to give him a call.

With butterflies in my stomach, I dialed the number where Gary worked. He didn't answer, so I left a message and explained my desire to give him copies of the photos Karen took of his team at the golf tournament and asked him to call me back. About an hour later, he called and we exchanged pleasantries over the phone. What he didn't know was that my heart skipped several beats the second I heard his voice. It was ridiculous how my body reacted. I maintained composure with my words and was confident he had no idea how nervous I was. Gary encouraged me to bring the photos by his office that afternoon and he'd give me a tour. When we hung up the phone, a smile jetted across my face and didn't leave the entire day. I felt giddy on the inside, like a teenager all over again!

Around 4:00 p.m., my friend and financial advisor, Bill Bandy, called and wanted to know if I could sign some papers. He arrived a few minutes before 5:00 and we exchanged small talk and then he asked me if I wanted to meet him and Gary Wells at a local fund raiser. Trying to hide my giddiness, I told Bill that I actually met Gary on Monday at a golf tournament and was headed to his office when I left work. Bill seemed quite surprised by my news. I decided that if Gary invited me to the fund raiser, that would be my 'go' sign and I'd attend. Bill and I walked to my car and I asked him about Gary and his late wife. Bill had nothing but kind things to say about Gary's wife, Jatawn, and he happened to have an audio CD of her sharing her experience with breast cancer in his car. He loaned me a copy of the CD.

As I listened to the audio CD of Jatawn speaking of her many battles with breast cancer, my heart was burdened. I couldn't help but feel badly for Gary and his two children for having endured the loss of his wife of twenty years, and their mother. I knew the feeling all too well as a child who'd lost her parents, but I didn't know what it was like to lose a spouse to death. Somehow, I felt better acquainted with Gary after listening to Jatawn's testimony on the way to his office. It seemed I had a better understanding of what kind of man Gary was after hearing the experience he'd been through.

I was a nervous wreck when I pulled into the bank parking lot, but determined to walk through this with faith believing God put Gary in my path just a few days prior. When Gary came downstairs to greet me, I remembered why I was giddy. There he stood with his distinguished gray hair, beautiful blue eyes and a smile that made my heart jump.

We hugged a nervous, quick hug and he gave me a brisk tour of the bank, then we headed upstairs to his office. I couldn't help but note that he wore boots and jeans. *Hmm....surely he dances country and western if he's dressed like that?* If he was nervous, he certainly didn't show it. His calm, self-assured demeanor was quite attractive to me. I, on the other hand, can hardly hide when I'm nervous since my port-wine birthmark on my neck turns beet red and my face usually follows suit. I hoped it was not a beacon while Gary and I talked.

I gave him the photos from the golf tournament and he set them on his book shelf where I noticed a family picture. He named everyone: his late wife Jatawn, his daughter, Bree and his son, Britton. *What a beautiful family.* After we exchanged more small talk, he asked if I would like to meet him and Bill Bandy at the fund raiser. *Oh! This is it! That's my sign.* As casually as I could muster, I said, "Sure. I'd love to meet you." He graciously walked me downstairs and said he'd see me over there. I could hardly wait.

My heart was so excited and yet so cautious. Palms were sweating, but I was determined to not mess this up. I also wanted to set good boundaries so I didn't fall over myself trying to impress him or make him like me. If it happened, it happened. If not, that was fine too. I already had respect for Gary just from the little I knew of him. For one thing, he stood by his wife's side while she battled with cancer over twelve years. He never left her. He was obviously a well-respected businessman in the community and an executive of a successful bank. It was difficult for me to not compare my past with his. When I did, a touch of shame tried to surface and I questioned if I deserved the opportunity to have a relationship with a man like him. I quickly had to dismiss those thoughts and keep moving forward in faith. *Don't go there Dawn.*

An affinity for Gary developed in my heart the day I met him. My first thoughts were, "Lord, I know I don't deserve a guy like Gary, but I desire to have a healthy relationship." I still struggled with issues of worthiness. The idea that I had the right to deserve anything good was foreign to me. Feelings of inadequacy don't die easily. My childhood memories were completely marred with dysfunction; I went through years of rebellion and I had one failed marriage under my belt. It was all I could do to put one foot in front of the other and trust that God was in control.

Thank goodness there were familiar faces at the fund raiser. Delighted to see Bill walk in, I made a bee-line for him. Within minutes, Gary arrived and joined us. Nervous small-talk ensued and others came up to visit with Gary, Bill or me. At one point, several conversations were going on at once.

In the background a country song played, so I asked Gary if he danced country and western. He confidently remarked, "Of course I do! I'm from Dumas." We laughed, and this opened the door for more questions. Within the course of a few minutes, we discovered we had many things in common. For instance, many years before, he'd obtained his private pilot's license and loved flying. I then explained that I grew up flying in a single-engine airplane with my dad. My mom also soloed as a pilot, but was never licensed. In fact, I'd taken fourteen hours of flying lessons, as well. We both found it interesting that we had that in common.

We each liked to run, dance, and the fact that we grew up seventeen miles apart was still amazing to both of us. We even shared the loss of a loved one to breast cancer. At one point, I thought he might be making up some of this to make a connection with me, but I realized he was not joking about any of it. *What are the odds, Lord?*

A few minutes later, a friend of mine who knew Shorty had back surgery asked how she was doing. I explained that she was great and had recovered one hundred percent. Gary overheard some of the conversation and asked what kind of dog I had. I said, "Oh, I have a Miniature Dachshund, named Shorty Danielle."

Gary nonchalantly remarked, "Oh yea? I do too. I have a Miniature Dachshund."

"What? You do *NOT* have a Miniature Dachshund! Get out!" I exclaimed with excitement and disbelief.

"No, seriously, I do have a Miniature Dachshund," Gary replied with a surprised look.

With skepticism, I asked, "Ok, what color is your dachshund?" I, being an avid Dachshund lover thought I might stump him with that question.

"He's a dapple," said Gary, still looking somewhat puzzled at my overreaction.

Knowing that dapple is an actual color for Dachshunds, I forged ahead with another question, trying to make certain this was the absolute truth. If it was-I was going to be in utter disbelief!

"Hmm? What's his name?" I questioned.

"Schnitzel," Gary calmly stated, looking confused.

"Well that is certainly a Dachshund name." I remarked in disbelief.

I adored my Dachshund, Shorty. It probably wasn't normal to the average person, but she was more like a child than a dog to me. The fact that Gary had a Miniature Dachshund himself was beyond my wildest dreams. It was a definite sign to me that he was the *one*. As crazy as that sounds, I just sensed it deep down. It was as if God gently said, "Dawn, I have someone so wonderful for you, he even has a Miniature Dachshund of his own." I couldn't help but ponder the idea that Gary might be the 'one' when it appeared he had so many of the characteristics on my list. But the fact he had a Dachshund absolutely sealed the deal for me. I realize that might be a strange sign to look for as a potential mate, but I just can't explain how I knew what I knew.

As the evening came to a close, Gary, Bill and I walked out together and said our good-byes in the parking lot. He mentioned he'd like to talk to me more about my mom and her battle with breast cancer and I suggested he call me, my number was in the phone book. Yes, I know, not exactly the best line, but it was all I could muster. Gary smiled and said he'd give me a call sometime. We hugged and retreated to our cars.

The minute I drove away, tears ran down my cheeks. Tears of joy. My heart knew Gary was the 'one' yet I was afraid to speak it out loud. All I said on the way home was, "Thank You, Lord! He has a Dachshund! *Are you kidding me?*"

Later that evening, Bill called me and confessed, "Dawn, I've been trying to introduce you to Gary for some time now. That's why I invited you to the banquet last week." I could hardly believe my ears. He and another mutual friend conspired to take us to lunch so we could 'accidentally' meet at the same restaurant. Bill was delighted we'd finally met.

There was no doubt how I felt about Gary after the night's events, and Bill heard the excitement in my voice. He assured me that Gary was interested and would call. I clung to his confidence and assurance and thanked him for caring for both of us.

I thought for certain that Gary would call that weekend, but God taught me patience instead. It seemed like an eternity but his call finally came the following Monday. When I heard his voice on the other end of the phone, I jumped up and down like a little girl. We decided since we would both be at a business function the next day, to meet for coffee afterwards. Although we neither mentioned the word 'date,' it seemed this was our first semi-unofficial date alone. The best word to describe my over all emotion was giddy even though I barely knew him. It all seemed too good to be true and every so often, a doubt crept up in my mind: *This guy is too good for you, Dawn. Once he finds out about your past, he'll bolt!*

It took every ounce of new faith I had to combat my doubts. I clung to the verse in II Corinthians 5:17- "Therefore, if anyone is in Christ he is a new creation; old things have passed away, behold, all things have become new" (NKJV). I believed I'd become a new person on February 23, 2003, but old thoughts continued to haunt me. There were plenty of people who'd argue my new-found righteousness. In fact, I still had doubts myself. However, I knew I didn't want to make the same relationship mistakes. Everything looked and felt differently than before.

Gary and I met at Starbuck's after the business function, but this time, the butterflies in my stomach had a boxing match in anticipation! I decided to bring a deck of cards to divert attention from my nervousness. I thought that if we played cards, the focus wouldn't be solely on each other the entire time. That would certainly relieve some pressure off me. You can learn a lot about a person in an hour of play. It turned out Gary loves to play Gin and we sat at a small table toward the back and talked for hours. We also played three games of Gin and I took him on two. (I suspect he let me win, though!)

When Gary so fondly spoke of his late wife, Jatawn, tears welled up in his eyes. It was refreshing to see a man express emotions like he did that night. That made a huge impact on me. I also had to wonder if our meeting was too soon; he was obviously still mourning the loss of his wife which was only eight months prior. I felt conflicted at times because I tend to want to fix any situation that brings pain to another, but there was no fixing this. Gary needed to walk through his grief in his own way and time, no matter how uncomfortable it was for me. I understood grief well and have learned it is different for everyone, but it's never easy to watch. Gary expressed to me he had no guilt or regrets and that Jatawn told him to go on and live his life abundantly. What a gift she gave him in that one sentence.

Throughout the evening, our conversation flowed comfortably; we laughed, we cried and most of all, we hoped. From my perspective, we'd come from opposite ends of the earth, yet, right now, right here, God put us together at this time in our lives. Gary had lived the past twenty years as a Godly, family man, raising his children and taking care of his wife as she battled cancer. I had lived a wild, party life, been divorced, had no children and had just surrendered my life to Jesus two years prior. It seemed improbable that we would have so much in common and feel so at ease with one another, but we did. Nothing ever felt forced and that was a welcomed new feeling.

While standing outside the coffee shop, Gary mentioned that he loved going to the movies, yet didn't ask me to go. He did, however, invite me to an open house the downtown bank branch was having two days later. I told him I'd try to make it. *Are you kidding? I will absolutely be there!* This time, I gave Gary my business card, since it had my cell phone number on it. I never wanted to miss his call. We gave each other a sweet hug and went our separate ways.

Everything inside and out was smiling. Giddiness took over my entire being and I could not stop thinking about Gary and a possible future with someone like him. This was all unchartered territory for me. I was a different person now, *a new person*-the old was gone. No longer did I want the party life and all that entailed. My dream was that I'd be a good wife someday and take care of my husband and our home. I knew God had great things for me and my future and I was anxious for it to present itself.

Desperately not wanting to ruin this great gift between Gary and me, I cried out to the Lord to save me from myself: *Lord, help me to be the friend Gary needs. Help me Lord, to put my selfish wants away. Help me to not go as fast as I have in the past with this relationship. Your will Lord, not mine.*

In the Lord's gentle way of speaking to me, I wrote down in my journal what I felt the Lord said: "Step back, Dawn and let Gary grieve. Don't try to stop his grieving process. Gary has healthy boundaries. That's a good thing. All is well."

Two days later, when I arrived at the bank open house, he was the first person I saw. A happy greeting and hug became our norm. Also there was our friend, Bill Bandy and another mutual friend, Charlie Cox. Charlie had a manner of embarrassing people in his not-so-subtle ways and he quickly picked up on the fact that Gary and I were a bit smitten with each other. Without warning, out of his mouth came, "Dawn, what's that on your neck? Did you let Gary give you a big hickey?" Everyone laughed, including me, but mine was a nervous, want-to-crawl-under-a-desk laugh. My face flushed to what I knew was a bright shade of red. This caused even more laughing, because my embarrassment was so evident. I went from an antique white to a blazing red in about two seconds, all in front of Gary and Bill. It took forever for the blood to retreat from my face. But we all enjoyed a good laugh. That was another important lesson I learned through my healing: not to take myself so seriously. It was much more fun to enjoy laughing at myself rather than feeling like a failure all the time.

Toward the end of the evening, Gary asked if I'd heard of the American Heart Association Ball, which was a local fund raising event. I said yes, I had, anxiously hoping his inquiry would lead to our first date.

"So, would you like to go to it this weekend?" Gary asked.

With butterflies in my stomach, I replied, "Sure, I'd love to."

Gary reached in his pocket and produced a ticket and said, "Okay, here's a ticket. Do you know where it's at? I can meet you there."

Okay, I must admit, I was just a little disappointed when he said he'd meet me there. Weren't you? That wasn't my hope for what I thought might be our first date, but I had to remember that this relationship looked different than any other I'd been involved with. God already told me that Gary had healthy boundaries and that was a good thing. I tried to hide any disappointment and went with the flow.

"Yes, I know where it's at. That'll be great! I'll meet you there at 7:30." I replied, wondering, *Was this really a date? No, I don't think I can officially call this a date.*

On the evening of the event, I decided I was glad that it wasn't our first official date. I was a nervous wreck just trying to figure out what to wear. I changed clothes five different times and finally settled on a brightly colored, floral sweater and white pants (no white shoes, though!). The agony it took to get to that point was enough to make me almost back out completely, but I needed to walk through this anxiety and fear. By the time I left my house, I thanked God Gary didn't pick me up. I needed the extra twenty minute drive to gain my composure after the grueling fashion trauma I put myself through.

With faith and confidence, I walked in and scanned the room looking for Gary, or any familiar face. He promptly found me. Gary and I hugged our usual hug.

I felt like the most blessed woman at the entire function. I was so proud to be there with Gary, even if we weren't on an official date. It was impossible for us to hide our feelings for each other. We *were* smitten.

We decided to leave the fund raiser and go dancing at a country bar with some other friends. Knowing I didn't want to two-step in heels, I decided to quickly drive home and change into my boots and jeans. I could hardly wait to dance with him.

Every minute I spent with Gary made the next minute easier and less nerve-wrecking. In every other relationship, I had alcohol to numb the anxious, insecure feelings I had around men. Now, with no alcohol, I could not escape any feeling I had; good or bad. My emotions were raw and this was such a new phenomenon for me; I wasn't sure how to act at times. I found that it was easiest to just be myself. The best I could surmise, Gary was interested and we both smiled the entire time we were together. I wanted to know him better and spend as much time with him as I could.

More than a year had passed since my last visit at a bar and it seemed odd to be going with this obviously righteous man, yet, it also seemed pure and innocent as well. All the information I'd gathered lead me to believe that Gary was not a heavy drinker and he could take it or leave it. I'd abused alcohol in the past so that was an important aspect to me to continue the relationship.

Gary and I danced until my feet ached, but I was not complaining. I had such a great time that night and especially enjoyed the slow songs we danced to. There was no lust between us and that gave me much peace. I couldn't help but notice his sweet, calm nature. He seemed so laid back and that was all very attractive to me.

At the end of the evening, I wasn't anxious about him trying to kiss me and therefore, not disappointed when he didn't. We promised each other we'd go dancing again since we both had such a great time. Then Gary said his famous parting last words, "I'll keep in touch." It's not exactly a phrase that sets a girls heart on fire. It sounded so non-committal and distant. Slowly but surely I learned what a healthy boundary resembled, and this was part of it.

During the hours I spent away from Gary, I thanked God fervently for all He'd shown me through the relationship with him. I'd already learned so much about healthy boundaries just in the few days I'd known Gary. I wanted a guy to pursue me, but I also had to be patient while I waited for his pursuit. It did come, though, and caused me to have greater respect and boundaries for myself and for Gary. This was all so new for me, but I loved every minute of it.

Gary's easy gentle manner balanced my easily excitable emotions and impulsiveness. It seemed crazy to think of marrying him so soon, but deep in my spirit, I knew he was the one. I felt at peace when I thought about being with him forever.

Gary asked me several times how I was still single. My explanation was complex. I felt I was still single because I'd just recently gotten closure on my divorce emotionally and I was still in the process of forgiving myself. I'm also very picky and somewhat high maintenance. He laughed at the thought of me being high maintenance, but I told him it was true, and I was not in denial about it (he can't say I didn't warn him).

Gary explained how he'd arrived to the place he was at emotionally from much advice from other widowers and he felt he'd been grieving for quite some time, even before Jatawn passed away. She'd struggled for years with cancer and they knew in advance it was terminal. He felt ready to move forward because Jatawn encouraged him to go and live abundantly; he carried no guilt. Having never lost a spouse to death, I couldn't relate, but he seemed so emotionally healthy, that I trusted where he was in the process of his grief.

Gary revealed to me that he'd told God he didn't want to have to tell his story to ten different women, in regards to dating. Gary asked God that if he met someone he should pay attention to, that the hair on the back of his neck would stand up. Gary confessed that the first day we met at the golf course, when I put my hand on his shoulder, the hair on the back of his neck stood up and he panicked and fled. That was music to my ears and assured me we were on the same path. *If he only knew the hours I spent questioning my every move that day he bolted!*

As the days went by, the more time I spent with Gary, the more I felt I was living in a dream. We communicated so easily with each other and I marveled at that. Communication was a very important characteristic to me in a prospective spouse because I knew it was imperative to any relationship's survival. I'd never communicated with someone of the opposite sex like I did with Gary.

One Saturday, we drove to Wheeler, Texas, about two hours away, where he and his dad own a ranch. I'd never been to Wheeler in all the years I'd lived in the Texas Panhandle, so when I saw the rolling green hills and trees everywhere, I couldn't believe it! The landscape was absolutely beautiful.

When we arrived at the ranch, his step-mother, Jerre was on the tractor and Jimmy, his dad, was nearby. Jerre reminded me of someone, a friend of mine named Carolyn Garner. It turned out, she and Carolyn are best friends! It seemed God had interwoven Gary and my lives for many years. Jimmy and Jerre were so gracious and kind and seemed genuinely excited for Gary and me. I'll never forget the warmth I felt from them and how it eased my anxiety.

At times, I still didn't feel I deserved a man like Gary. Little claws of shame clung to my heart. Every time I met someone in Gary's camp, I feared they would think the same thing-*she doesn't deserve him.* It's so difficult to get rid of every fiber of shame, but I kept pressing on, putting one foot in front of the other. I wanted a different life than I'd had in the past and I needed to stay close to God to remind myself that I was a new person in Him, not based on anything I'd done, but simply by His grace alone.

When Gary and I left Wheeler, I felt more secure in our relationship having met Jimmy and Jerre. I had a connection with them right away and I was so grateful for that. Our next stop was Norm and Karen's house for a party with Karen's friends from out of town. Gary met Norm and Karen for the second time since the golf tournament but this particular night, the entire family was there. Without any hesitation, Gary fit right in. One thing I noticed early on was that I wasn't worried about Gary while at Norm and Karen's. I didn't need to stand by his side every minute to make sure he was comfortable and had a good time. He carried himself so well and with such confidence. He didn't wait for me to take the lead; he took it on his own. That was an immense weight lifted off my shoulders. In past relationships, I had a sense of false responsibility and feared my date wouldn't have a good time. I assumed responsibility for their emotions and well-being. That is a prime characteristic of codependency, and one I was thrilled to leave behind.

At the end of our evenings, standing in my driveway seemed to be our spot for saying goodnight but that particular night was special. When Gary leaned in to kiss me goodnight, I didn't pull away. My knees about buckled. The significance of that kiss substantiated what I'd already determined — I was going to marry this guy. I knew it in my heart.

# Chapter Twelve

## *Trust is not for Wimps*

No doubt, I was falling in love with Gary. This relationship was one of the best things that had happened in my life. I could hardly believe it was happening to me. At times, I still worried I didn't deserve Gary. He was unlike anyone I'd ever dated and the lack of familiarity caused me to doubt. Anxiety rose as I thought about us getting more seriously involved and having to explain all the horrible mistakes I'd made in my past - and there were plenty. My greatest fear was that Gary would walk away after hearing some of the things I'd done. I realized everyone has a past, but for others my age, that sort of wild-living past is usually several years removed, not just a stone's throw away. I thought I hadn't been a follower of Christ long enough to deserve Gary's love. Grace was a difficult concept for me to grasp as an immature Christian. I knew I was light years away from where I'd been, and thankful for that, but certainly not where Gary had been for the past twenty years. I was afraid the gap might be too much for us to overcome.

More than ever, I had to trust God's timing. Doubt and worry were two evils that continued to tempt my thoughts. You should have heard some of the ridiculous conversations I had in my mind. Some days it was all I could do not to grow weak from the mind games I played with myself. I'd lived many years of my life pretending to be happy, and now I had a shot at the real thing. I wasn't about to give that up without a good fight.

As our relationship continued to become more serious, I could no longer delay the inevitable conversation I needed to have with Gary. I never wanted him to hear anything derogatory about me from someone else. Through many prayers and tears, I gathered as much courage as I could before I spoke to him. For days, my stomach churned and I was nauseated at the thought of Gary's possible reaction. I was terrified that what I had to tell him would be a deal breaker for him and he'd walk away. My old abandonment and rejection fears surfaced again and I fought them off as hard as I could. I clung to my ounce of faith and asked God to give me the words.

Finally it was time. One evening, as Gary sat across from me I told my story – with all the humiliating and demoralizing details. There was a pause, and to my utter amazement, he didn't even flinch. He looked me straight in the eye and said, "Dawn, I have a past, too. Who am I to throw the first stone? From the first day I met you I saw a pure heart and I still see a pure heart today."

A wave of relief started at my head and washed over my entire body. Tears streamed down my face in awe of his reaction. No matter what I said, I couldn't convince him how bad I was before because he never knew that person. He couldn't even visualize what I told him, but every morsel of it was true, unfortunately. God saw my new heart and now Gary saw my new heart; yet I still I struggled to see it for myself. My past still had claws stuck in me, but a few of them were plucked out that night as Gary silently expressed an unconditional love and acceptance for me. I'd punished myself repeatedly for my past mistakes and thought I deserved punishment from Gary as well, but he offered nothing but grace. I'd never experienced anything like that in my life, but I knew that I longed for more of it. The closer I got to Gary the more I realized what God intended a healthy relationship to resemble.

****

With the worst behind us, I felt we could move forward. It was time to meet his two children. One evening at a fundraiser, I met Gary's twenty year old daughter, Bree. When I first laid eyes on her, my immediate thought was, "Wow! She is absolutely beautiful!" I wondered if she was as nervous to meet me as I was her. Gary spoke so highly of her and all her accomplishments. I wasn't surprised that she was as beautiful on the inside as she was on the outside, but how could she not be with a father like Gary?

Later that same evening, Gary and I dropped by his house and I met Britton, his seventeen-year-old son. His charismatic personality shined through during our brief encounter. I sincerely hoped there was a future for all of us together, even though, I knew that right now might be too soon for Bree and Britton since they were still grieving the death of their mother.

I continued to meet members of Gary's family. His mom, JoMarie and stepdad, Bill also seemed delighted that Gary had met someone. JoMarie and I both loved the subject of psychology and she is currently a counselor. Bill was one of the kindest persons I'd ever met, with such a great sense of humor. I also met Gary's grandfather and grandmother, Papa Joe and Flo. Everyone in Gary's family seemed so grateful that Gary was not alone. They had walked the difficult journey with him and Jatawn for many years. Gary had an abundance of family and I was running short, so my heart was delighted to meet all of them.

Each day, I searched God for His will concerning the relationship with Gary. After two months of exercising healthy boundaries, our relationship continued to blossom. It all took some getting used to, but was well worth it. I continued to put my trust in God and believed that everything was happening according to His schedule, not mine. Gary and I continued to spend time with Bree and Britton. This was all foreign territory for each of us. At the end of my prayers, I thanked God for finding me worthy to be in Gary's life, and his children's life. It was a huge honor to me. I continued to pinch myself to make sure this wasn't all a dream...*it wasn't.*

One day Gary spoke the four words that caused my heart to melt, "I love you, Dawn." It was music to my ears as those words often reached the tip of my own tongue numerous times before, but I was determined to wait for Gary to say them first. Finally, I felt able to relax in his arms; all the tension and worry and wondering vanished. It was a magical moment. We agreed we were committed to each other but I still could not believe this was happening to me. *Me, Lord, You picked me to be with Gary? It seems too good to be true!*

Every day that passed, his unconditional love became more and more real to me. I don't think I've ever been loved like that in my life. My heart overflowed with gratefulness for this beautiful man and that God picked *me* to cherish him and love him in return.

August that year arrived with all its sweltering heat. We celebrated Gary's 43rd birthday on August third. Since our initial meeting on April 25th, so much had transpired in our relationship. In three short months, we began dating, met family and friends, and fell deeply in love. It all seemed so fast, yet right on schedule.

As wonderful as everything was, there seemed to be an invisible wall we kept running into. The one year anniversary of Jatawn's death was quickly approaching August 19. The wall I felt wasn't a massive obstruction, but I sensed its presence. I hoped that after the one year anniversary, that barrier would fade away. The build up to the anniversary date was extremely hard on Gary, his family and friends, and certainly understandable. At the same time, it was difficult for me to find my place in situations when I knew Jatawn's loved ones grieved her death so deeply. My codependent nature wanted to fix their hurts and wrap my arms around them. But I had to learn to allow them to grieve in their own way and not try to stop their pain. Pain is individual and inevitable for everyone. Walking through pain is what causes us to grow and heal. I needed to allow that process to happen naturally no matter how uncomfortable I was in awkward situations.

August nineteenth came and Gary spent the day with Bree and Britton and Jatawn's family. As the minutes ticked away, I thought of each of them and their sorrow. My heart ached for them that day. Death had visited my family too many times and I knew the kind of pain they were experiencing. Jatawn was much too young to die at the age of forty.

As the anniversary date passed, I felt a gentle sigh of relief. It was difficult for everyone, yet we all survived and seemed relieved the day was behind us. Knowing Jatawn was dancing with the angels in Heaven brought a sense of peace to everyone, I believe.

I felt that invisible wall softly fade away as Gary and I continued to grow closer. His ability to communicate his emotions, desires and dreams amazed me. I'd never met a man that could communicate so effortlessly. He was certainly a breath of fresh air in my life.

Gary and I started to have conversations about getting married. When? Where? Who to invite? Big wedding or small? One day, Gary nonchalantly asked me what kind of engagement ring I'd like. He didn't trust his ability to choose a ring for me, so he solicited my input. He made it clear that his formal proposal would come sometime after he purchased the ring, and would be a surprise.

I revealed my favorite rings to Gary and soon realized, he hadn't shopped much for jewelry. The expression on his face when I showed him the price of a loose diamond was, well . . . priceless! (We still laugh about that today). We ordered the ring I found that I liked. It was absolutely beautiful. The wait for the proposal began and seemed to go on forever. I wondered how Gary might surprise me, but certainly had no definitive ideas. I constantly looked for clues for over a month. My obsessive personality was getting the best of me!

I loved going to the ranch in Wheeler because I could run around in sweats and no makeup and feel like I was on the farm. One particular weekend in late October was no different. Britton, Bree and their friends joined us to celebrate Britton's birthday. While Bree and I cooked dinner, Gary decided he wanted to sit in one of the deer blinds to see the wildlife. Knowing how much he loves to hunt, I didn't think anything of it. Britton and his friends left the house without my knowledge as Bree and I were engrossed in some girl talk while we prepared dinner. Bree stepped out of the kitchen for a few minutes, and then returned with a greeting card. For a moment, I thought it was from her, but she informed me that it was from Gary. I opened it up and Gary wrote instructions for me to join Bree and proceed to the pond area. There, I would find my next set of instructions. Bree smiled her big, beautiful smile and I suspected the proposal was imminent. My heart beat quickly as we drove to the pond. *Oh Lord! This is really it, isn't it?*

There at the pond, stood Britton and his friends with a long-stemmed rose and another card with instructions for me. Bree stayed with Britton at the pond, and I proceeded alone to the creek which was about half a mile away. Bree and Britton helped Gary plan his surprise and I was delighted they wanted to be a part of our proposal. When I arrived at the bridge, a sign hung across the entry of the bridge that said, "Stop! Walk across the bridge and wait at the picnic table for a surprise!" There, across the way, twelve long-stemmed roses waited for me in a beautiful vase. I couldn't see Gary anywhere, but I knew he was near. My heart was pounding with anticipation and joy. Out from behind a large cottonwood tree stepped my knight in shining armor – except he wore a sport jacket, tie, jeans and hunting boots! Gary walked over to me and held my hand. Staring into each other's eyes, neither of us could stop smiling.

Gary got down on one knee, and looked up at me with his beautiful, blue eyes and asked, "Dawn, will you marry me?" He presented the ring that we'd picked out over a month ago. It was just as gorgeous as I remembered.

Without hesitation, I said "Yes! I will!" Gary quickly stood up and we embraced and laughed and held each other tightly for a long time. I knew this was the man God hand-picked for me and I could hardly believe the proposal had finally arrived. No doubt, Gary surprised me!

Later that night, unable to believe the events of the day, I lay in bed for hours before going to sleep. My heart jumped with joy at the idea of marrying Gary and now it was official. I thanked God repeatedly, knowing Gary was a gift from Him. Even with all my imperfections, God made it possible for this man to love and cherish me. I knew I loved Gary tremendously and was committed to being the best wife I could possibly be through God's grace.

\*\*\*\*

Before we knew it, the holidays were upon us. The year before, I'd spent Thanksgiving with Norm and Karen and their family and thoroughly enjoyed myself. In the past, being single was difficult this time of year and I dreaded the holidays. I rarely knew with whom or where I'd spend that time and it left me with a feeling of angst, but the last couple of years were so different.

Gary had a large family between his dad and step mom, Jimmy and Jerre, his mom and step dad, JoMarie and Bill, his grandparents, Papa Joe and Flo and Jatawn's parents, Archie and Judy in Dumas. After an afternoon visit to JoMarie and Bill's house, we headed to Norm and Karen's house for Thanksgiving dinner and it was a joyful evening. Norm and Karen were so happy that I'd found someone as wonderful as Gary to be with for the rest of my life. That Thanksgiving was one I'll never forget.

Before we blinked, Christmas was upon us. Gary and Jatawn were married twenty years, and every Christmas, they went to Dumas and spent the holiday with Jatawn's parents. This year marked the second year without Jatawn, and the first year with me. Although I was invited to come to Dumas and spend the night with them, I was extremely uncomfortable about that idea. Once again, my insecurities rose to the top. If ever I felt I didn't belong somewhere, it was at Jatawn's parent's house on Christmas Eve while engaged to Gary. I appreciated the invitation, and knew it was given in all sincerity, but I politely declined the offer.

As agreed, I drove up to Dumas Christmas morning to be with Gary and the kids. I thought my presence had to be very awkward for all involved and especially for me. My perception of what others thought of me didn't help matters either. I felt that I was the only one in the room that didn't 'belong.' I worried my presence made them miss Jatawn even more. Too fearful to risk the disapproval of anyone, I went along, but it wasn't easy. My saving grace was how kind and loving Judy and Archie were to me. It was as if they'd known me forever. No matter how insecure I felt on the inside, they made the experience much less painful by welcoming me with open arms.

Yet, the fact that I was Gary's second wife, not his first, played into my insecurity of feeling like a second-best. It was very similar to how I felt when I was younger. I now struggled to feel good enough compared to Gary's first wife. What didn't help matters was my compulsion to compare myself to Jatawn. Comparisons are the breeding ground for insecurities. There was still work for God to do in my heart and my discomfort made it obvious.

After the holidays Gary and I found a house to buy that sat across the street from Jimmy and Jerre, his dad and step mom. I was absolutely delighted! Jimmy and Jerre welcomed me with open arms and continued to open their lives to me throughout our engagement, offering their help any way they could for the wedding arrangements. The idea of living across the street from them seemed to make them just as content as it did us. When Gary and I walked into that house for the first time, peace came over me. *This will be our first home together.*

A few days later, I put a For Sale sign in the front yard of my house and two days after that signed a contract and sold it. Gary got a call from a local banker who heard he was getting married and asked if he wanted to sell his house. They came to look and before they left, made Gary an offer to buy! Gary never even put a For Sale sign in the yard. We were amazed at how God opened doors and caused things to happen in our favor. It all seemed like a beautiful dream coming true right before our eyes.

I moved into our new house in January 2006. Gary and Britton remained in their home in Canyon. Britton was about to graduate from high school in May and Bree was graduating from Texas A&M. Our wedding was set for the end of May so needless to say it was stacking up to be a full month with several celebrations at hand! Everyone was excited.

# Chapter
# Thirteen
*Darkest Just Before the Dawn*

All our plans and preparations progressed smoothly as the first few days in May arrived. Then one evening, around 10:00 pm, Gary got a call on his cell phone from a policeman. The policeman asked Gary to come to his mom's home immediately. Thankfully, JoMarie and Bill only lived about a mile from our new house, although they were set to move the next day to a smaller condominium they'd purchased.

Gary and I had no idea what it was all about, so we rushed over to their home. We arrived just minutes later, walked past the policemen, and saw JoMarie come toward us, crying hysterically. "Bill is dead! Oh my God!" We were stunned and speechless.

Through her sobbing, JoMarie was able to communicate that she was at Bill's shop about thirty minutes prior and headed home in her vehicle and Bill was to follow soon after. They planned to have a glass of wine to celebrate their move the next day, but he never made it home. Shortly after JoMarie got home, a policeman arrived to tell her the tragic news. Bill's small car was hit on the driver's side by a speeding motorcyclist and he was killed instantly.

Gary and I were both in complete shock upon hearing that Bill was dead. Throughout their large home, sat boxes packed full of all their belongings. The mover was to be there at 9:00 a.m. the next morning. It all seemed impossible that Bill was gone, simply impossible.

To know Bill Brown for one minute was to love him. He loved the Lord so much and it showed through his countenance and his actions. He'd been involved in a prison ministry for years and everyone who knew Bill truly adored him. He overflowed with life and vigor and even loved riding motorcycles himself. It made no sense that he died so suddenly and was no longer with us.

Gary and I joined JoMarie on the couch and held her as she sobbed. My heart broke for her. After Gary's parents divorced, JoMarie thought she'd never marry again. She was perfectly content to be single and had convinced her family she would remain single forever. Then, she met precious Bill. A mutual friend introduced them after he'd lost his wife to a terminal illness. They dated around five years before marrying. It was obvious they adored one another by their sweet glances and acts of service to each other.

The reality of what happened that night finally hit around midnight. JoMarie was exhausted from the shock of the news and the impact it had on her body, mentally and physically. It was more than she could bear. We encouraged her to lie down in her bed to rest and she finally did.

Gary and I prepared for the next day and began notifying family. The events of the evening were surreal. All gears shifted from celebrating the upcoming graduations and our wedding, to finding an interim apartment for JoMarie, putting her and Bill's belongings in storage and planning the funeral of a beloved man.

The next three days blurred together and finally culminated at the beautiful service that honored Bill's noble life on Earth. The church was full of his many friends who over the years had grown to know and love him. My eyes blurred from stinging tears as I saw the brokenness of JoMarie. I'd attended many funerals in my lifetime, but never my husband's and I could not even fathom that kind of loss. There are some times when sorrow is inconsolable and this was such a time.

God had done a miraculous healing in my life, but I still struggled with a false sense of responsibility for others hurts or needs. The anguish I felt for JoMarie's suffering was more than I could bear at times. In my heaviness, I began to pressure myself to be the best wife, stepmother, daughter-in-law, employee, sister, niece and friend; it struck me like an unsuspecting tidal wave. With the heavy grief and shock of Bill's death, the graduations, moving Bree home, to our upcoming wedding, I was overwhelmed. I found myself on my knees begging God to help me juggle all the roles I'd signed up for.

In the midst of this tragedy, my precious Aunt Sandra had just completed several rounds of chemotherapy and radiation to treat her lung cancer. Sandra lived in Sunray and was one of my dad's four sisters who helped care for me after Mom left. I loved Sandra dearly. We all thought the cancer was in remission, when not long after Bill died, tests showed the cancer was now in her liver. I did not think I could handle one more word of heartbreaking news.

One week later, as some of the dust settled, Gary and I traveled to College Station to attend Bree's graduation from Texas A&M. With all the pomp and circumstance from an incredible university, Bree proudly walked across the stage and received her diploma for four years of hard work and dedication. It was a great diversion from all the sadness we'd experienced in recent days.

After packing up Bree's apartment and loading all her belongings in a U-Haul truck, Gary and I began the long road back to Amarillo. Along the way, Karen called me to inform me that Norm had become ill with flu-like symptoms and she took him to the emergency room. His kidney had not been functioning well for the past few months. The emergency room doctor knew Norm was a special case because of his transplanted kidney and suggested Karen take him to Lubbock so his doctors could monitor him.

When they arrived in Lubbock, it was determined from his symptoms that his body was rejecting the kidney and the best option was to remove it. The surgery was low-risk since the kidney sat just below the skin and could be easily removed. When Karen relayed this information to me, my first reaction was disbelief that I was receiving the sad news that Norm had to undergo another surgery. *Lord? How much can one person take?* At this point, Norm had four kidneys in his body: his two kidneys, and two transplanted kidneys. Yet, none were functioning. Karen assured me that the doctors felt this was the best thing to do to counteract Norm's rejection of the kidney. I felt some temporary relief after talking with Karen that Norm would be fine through the surgery, so I told her I'd call her the next day when we arrived in Amarillo.

Up to this point, I'd lived a fully surrendered life to Jesus for about three years and every day, my faith either grew, or was attacked by doubts – there was no middle ground. I explained to Gary the situation with Norm but hid my worry and fear deep inside. I wanted to believe there was no risk involved with Norm's upcoming surgery, but it stands to reason that every surgery has some risk involved. The negative thoughts diminished when I recalled all the medical problems Norm endured over the last seven years. No matter the issue, Norm triumphed through all of them. He was a strong, courageous man who'd been through much worse than this. I tried to convince myself that Norm was going to be fine and the surgery would be non-eventful.

Upon arriving in Amarillo, I learned from Karen that the surgery itself went well, but there was a complication afterward. Norm was bleeding internally. The doctors went back into surgery to cauterize the bleeding arteries and closed him up again. His condition over the next few days stabilized somewhat, but he remained in ICU.

In the midst of driving to Lubbock to be with Norm, Karen and their family, I was also trying to help transition JoMarie into an apartment while the condo was being remodeled. We first found an apartment across the street from her condo that was an ideal location. After getting JoMarie settled into that apartment, it did not take her long to realize the apartment complex was not a safe place to live and with her frail state, the last thing we all wanted was for her to feel unsafe. We got her moved to another apartment that was newer and much safer. My heart broke for the grief she was experiencing. At times, I knew it was almost unbearable for her and it seemed all I had to offer were feeble prayers to comfort her.

Just when I made it back to work and things seemed like they might calm down, I received a call from Karen that Norm's condition had worsened overnight. His blood pressure was dipping so low, the doctors thought they'd lost him. Again, his arteries were bleeding and that was causing the low dips in blood pressure. They decided to take him back to surgery again. I felt I needed to be there so I explained the situation to my manager and she agreed I should go to Lubbock, immediately.

By the time I arrived, Norm was out of surgery and in fair condition. They put him on a ventilator so he wouldn't strain to breathe on his own, nor would there be a chance of losing him if his blood pressure sank too low. Norm was in the hospital almost ten days and his condition was up and down like a roller coaster, as were all of our emotions. Karen and Kendra had set up camp in a tiny family conference room and this was where everyone gathered. Norm's case attracted numerous doctors as they all conferred together to determine his best treatment options.

Dr. Van Buren, Norm's surgeon for our transplant, and our friend, explained to me that Norm's arteries and veins resembled those of an eighty-year-old from years of dialysis. They were weak and didn't heal like those of a healthy person. That news was devastating to hear because I knew there was no remedy.

From the three different surgeries, Norm's body had encountered much physical stress, not to mention the side-effects of the immunosuppressant drugs he'd been on for many years. All of his organs suffered some effect from the drugs, the dialysis and the lack of kidney function. Karen, Kendra and I prayed fervently to God believing He could heal Norm.

In my weary state from all that transpired from the beginning of May, the enemy came to torment me with all sorts of negative thoughts. The longer Norm lay in that hospital, the more I felt that my kidney failed him and didn't give him a healthy life, as I'd so deeply hoped it would. Looking back, those thoughts don't even seem rational now, but at the time they were absolute torture. As a new Christian, I quickly learned the enemy is relentless and continues to kick us when we're down.

The battle was on, and I was already weary from Bill's death, Sandra's cancer and now Norm's condition. It felt as if rocks were falling on top of me from a cliff and if the rocks didn't kill me from the blows, I'd be buried alive underneath them. There didn't seem to be any light at the end of the tunnel and I prayed fervently for God to help me and show me what to do next. As I poured out my requests to Him, I anxiously waited for His answer.

My heart hurt so badly for Karen and Kendra and Kyle and yet I was helpless. My prayers seemed like whispers of air that dissipated once the words left my lips. The claws of depression sunk into my skin and I was too weak and weary to fight it off.

Over the next few days, I drove back and forth to Lubbock to be with Norm, Karen and their family. We all believed Norm was going to come home before the wedding and walk me down the aisle. On some days, Norm's condition was stable and the next day, it quickly deteriorated. There was no rhyme or reason and the doctors were baffled as well, which offered us no comfort.

One Sunday, while standing and worshiping at church, I had an anxiety attack. Out of nowhere, sweat beaded up on my forehead and I was burning up! I heard the music in the background like an echo and every time I blinked my eyes, total blackness was all I saw for a few seconds. My heart raced. Nausea hit me like a tidal wave and I sat down in my chair thinking I was about to get sick or pass out - I wasn't sure which. My mouth watered and I prayed, *Oh Lord, please don't let me get sick or pass out. Please let this moment pass. Calm me down Lord, calm me down.* Gary asked if I was all right and grabbed my hand, which was cold and clammy. Barely through a whisper, I told him what just happened and I couldn't stand up again, I needed some time. After a few minutes, the nausea passed and my body returned to its normal temperature. I no longer felt faint or dizzy and knew I'd weathered the storm. The episode frightened me because I didn't know what the physical cause was. It didn't take a rocket scientist to discover the mental cause – my world was crashing all around me and there was nothing I could do.

I realized the pressure was too great for me anymore. My life seemed to be going a thousand different directions. Gary and I decided that I'd temporarily quit my job until we got everything and everyone settled, from our wedding, to the kids, to JoMarie and all our loved ones who were ill. Walking away from my job was difficult. I'd been independent for many years of my life and took great pride in providing for myself. While I'd never been a career-minded person, eager to climb the corporate ladder, I did like the freedom of making my own money and I loved sales. I wrestled with the decision and prayed about it diligently. Repeatedly I heard God say, "I want you to be Gary's healthy wife." At the time, I didn't feel very healthy, physically or mentally. Resigning seemed to be the best thing for what was happening in our life at that time.

The day before the wedding, I was in Amarillo to receive some out of town guests and family over at Jimmy and Jerre's house. I still believed Norm was going to be okay. I convinced myself all would work out. Around seven that evening, Kendra called to tell me to pray; Norm was not doing well and it didn't look good. In my despair, I sank to my knees in Jimmy and Jerre's living room and wept at the thought of losing Norm. I could not wrap my head around what all had happened the past three weeks.

We all prayed right then for Norm and his family and that God would intervene.

In an instant, the atmosphere again went from one of celebration of an upcoming wedding to sadness and despair. No longer able to keep up the facade, I decided to go on home, which, thankfully, was just across the street. Gary, along with Scott and Sheila his brother and sister-in-law, joined me. When some of our friends heard the news, they came over too. The mood was solemn and quiet and then my phone rang again; it was Kendra. Desperate to hear something good, I knew immediately after hearing her voice, it was not good.

"Dawn, he's gone. Daddy's gone," Kendra whispered through her sobbing. My tears flowed like a gushing water well. For the past two weeks, the fear of losing Norm was in the back of mind, even though I wanted to believe he would be at the wedding even if he couldn't walk me down the aisle.

"I'm so sorry Kendra. I am so sorry. I can't believe it, I just can't," I said.

"I know, I can't either. But he's not in any pain now. No more suffering; I'll have Mom call you when we get home tonight." Kendra gently uttered. With that, we hung up. There were no words that could console either of us, so there was no need to stay on the phone. Words can't even describe the ache I felt in my heart for Karen and her family, and even myself. It was impossible to believe that this towering man who stood six feet seven inches with his booming baritone voice could possibly not be with us anymore. As my cheeks burned with hot tears, I kept shaking my head back and forth in disbelief. *Lord, I can't believe he's gone.*

Gary held me tightly as he tried to comfort me. We both knew grief all too well and he knew there were no words that could take the pain away. I wondered out loud if Gary and I should even get married the next day. *How can we?* It didn't even seem possible to me at that point. How on Earth could I walk down the aisle knowing Norm is gone and Karen and her family are suffering their greatest loss ever? I honestly did not know what to do. Everyone convinced me that of course Gary and I would get married the next day. Norm had been thrilled for us and he wouldn't want our marriage to be placed on hold. I wasn't entirely convinced myself.

It was almost midnight when everyone, including Gary, departed. My phone rang and much to my delight, I heard Karen's voice on the other end. In her unbelievably strong and faithful way, she encouraged me that I was absolutely going to get married the next day because Norm would have it no other way. He loved Gary and wanted us to be together and she and the kids would all be there. I was shocked that in their grief they would even consider attending. Karen went on to tell me they would not miss the wedding for anything. Karen's faith and strength inspired me beyond measure and I knew I could marry Gary the next day. I was completely awestruck by Karen's faith and courage. She had been through so much with Norm's health over the past seven years, and through it all, her faith was stronger than ever. Through Karen, God's strength was infused into my broken heart that night. In some miraculous way, I envisioned myself walking down the aisle in the decorated church, despite the heaviness of my heart.

# Chapter
# Fourteen
*Where Are You God?*

The next morning, my eyes opened slowly and I peered around the room. This was the day of my wedding, as bittersweet as it was. I would marry Gary and have the dream God long ago promised me. It was hard to absorb what happened less than twenty-four hours before; the reality of Norm's death became more concrete with each moment. It was all I could do at times to go through the motions that day.

Thankfully, two dear girlfriends came and helped me get dressed and fix my hair. Usually, makeup and hair are two extremely important details of a bride's wedding day, but I had no energy for either. With their help, I looked the part, despite my sadness and tears.

After my friends left, I kneeled on my bathroom floor and cried out to God to help me get through the day. My heart was broken, yet I was about to marry the man of my dreams. More than anything, my heart ached for Karen and her family's loss and the fact there was nothing I could do to help ease their pain. Only God could get us through a day such as this.

The church filled with friends and family while I waited in the Bridal room for the ceremony to begin. My close girlfriends and sister, Tanya, joined me and most didn't know we'd lost Norm the night before. Every time we explained what happened, the sadness that came over them, spilled over to me and I continued to cry. I reapplied makeup that had smeared down my cheeks numerous times. My legs were shaky and weak and I seriously wondered if I could physically stand for the entire ceremony. I peeked out the window of the Bridal suite which looked to the front of the church and saw Karen, and her entire family, walk in. A peace enveloped me upon seeing them. Within minutes, Karen and Kendra courageously appeared at the door of the Bridal suite. Not many hours before, they were at Norm's side as he drifted away to be with the Lord. Now, they were here, to attend my wedding. There were no words that could be spoken, just long embraces and many tears between us. Karen's strength illuminated her eyes and smile. Her strength gave me the courage to walk down that aisle with my head held high as she and I both knew how delighted Norm was that I was going to marry Gary.

Gary and I decided the night before that he would address our loss of Norm before I came down the aisle. As I stood at the closed doorway and saw him through the small window, I could barely hear him, but what I did hear was so precious and gracious. Most everyone there had no idea of Norm's recent surgery and subsequent complications from it. Needless to say, they were aghast to hear he'd passed away just the night prior. Gary read a scripture that God showed me the day before: Psalm 118:5-6 (NKJV) *In my anguish I cried to the Lord, and He answered by setting me free. The Lord is with me; I will not be afraid.* Gary went on to add a verse close to his heart, Psalm 118: 24 (NKJV) *This is the day the Lord has made; let us rejoice and be glad in it.* Gary asked everyone to grab the hand next to them and join him in prayer. I was so proud of his graciousness and ability to stand confidently and handle this difficult situation with such poise and humility.

The beautiful instrumental Wedding March began and the double doors opened. My heart ached to have Norm there with me, to escort me down the aisle. With weak knees, I walked the first few steps as Gary strode gallantly toward me. It seemed like eternity until he reached for my arm and led me to the altar. As I smiled weakly at my friends and family standing to honor us, tears ran down my cheeks. I saw the shock in their faces at the thought of losing Norm the night before. One minute I felt guilty for smiling because my heart hurt so badly for Karen and her family and the next minute, I felt guilty for crying because this was Gary and my wedding day and I should be rejoicing! My emotions were all over the board and, I could hardly pay attention to what Pastor Bo said during the ceremony. As Pastor Bo conducted the ceremony, we faced our friends and family and I could not help but glance over to Karen and her family. There they all sat on the front row, steadfast. It was an absolute miracle for them to be there, celebrating with us, while deep inside, mourning the loss of Norm. I could not even guess what they were feeling or thinking, just as no one could understand what I was feeling or thinking. The last place I wanted to be was at an altar for all eyes to be on me while I was in the midst of one of the most sorrowful days of my life - which just happened to also be my wedding day. I did not have the ability to separate the two. It was beyond surreal. After our vows were repeated, communion taken and the announcement of "Mr. and Mrs. Gary Wells"; finally, a sigh of relief came out as we headed down the aisle as husband and wife. I was so thankful the ceremony was behind us; that was the most difficult aspect of the entire day.

Afterward, we took photographs with family and then hurried to the reception down the hallway where all our friends patiently awaited our arrival. Because of my love of wedding cake, a sincere smile appeared on my face when we entered the reception hall and there stood our beautiful cake. (No doubt, I was in desperate need for some comfort food). We rushed through the usual wedding pictures where the bride and groom feed each other a piece of cake and as promised, we didn't smear any on each other's faces. Today just wouldn't have been the day.

The song we chose to dance our first dance to was *God Blessed the Broken Road* by Rascal Flatts. On one of our early dates while out dancing, we had the pleasure of dancing to that particular song and the words rang so true for both of us, we decided to deem it our wedding song. *God blessed the broken road that led me straight to you.* Both of our hearts had been broken before we met, yet we emphatically agreed that God blessed that brokenness that led us to each other.

As thankful as I was that everyone came to our wedding and shared their Memorial Day weekend with us, I was never so ready to depart an event as I was that day. Physically, I felt I'd run a marathon. (I've never actually run a marathon, but I think that's how I would feel if I had). The internal stress from the roller coaster effect of my emotions had taken such a toll and I was beyond exhausted. We had plans to fly out that afternoon to Los Angeles for the night, then on to Hawaii the next day.

We left little time between the reception and our departing flight so we dashed home, changed clothes and were off again to the airport. As I sat on the plane and penned the day's events, it still seemed unbelievable to me. There was no doubt; my life would never be the same. Nor would Karen's, I thought. More than ever, I needed God to show me who He was. I knew He was the God of the Universe and was larger than any trial or scheme the devil sent my way. I needed His protection from the enemy in my weakened state because I'd grown too weary to battle him. The word that kept swirling through my mind was "bittersweet." Norm went to the highest glory of all, next to the Lord in Heaven forever, and the next day, I walked down the aisle and joined my life with my new husband. Bittersweet, indeed.

In some ironic way, I felt Norm was right in the midst of us. I wouldn't have been at the Kidney Foundation Golf tournament that day and met Gary, if it hadn't been for Norm. My deepest desire was to give Norm twenty-five more years to live with the donation of my kidney, but that was not to be. One thing I was certain about was that I had experienced the greatest blessing through Norm, his family and his love. Only having him in my life for a short time gave me a lifetime benefit.

Our honeymoon destination was Maui, Hawaii and at times, I could not believe I was even on a honeymoon. Gary and I prepaid for everything months in advance, but it crossed my mind that I shouldn't go on a honeymoon because I would miss Norm's funeral. The precious woman who videotaped our wedding, was also going to tape Norm's funeral service for us. Karen insisted that Gary and I take the honeymoon as planned.

I've been through some traumatic events in my life, but I'd never felt so perplexed by a situation like this and had no idea how to react. I desperately wanted to be with Gary on our honeymoon, but I could not stop thinking about Karen and her family. The relentless attacks on my emotions had been ongoing since the beginning of May. God gave me what I needed to get through each day, not two days, but each day-one at a time.

When I spoke with Karen, her strength resonated through the phone, and I got a boost of faith. More than anything, I wanted her to be okay. It felt so wrong that I was beginning my journey in life with a wonderful man and her journey with Norm just ended. That seemed so unfair to me and it was difficult to be joyous.

I never dreamed I'd be grieving so deeply while on my honeymoon, but I was. Gary knew firsthand about grief and he faithfully comforted me as best he could. No one completely understood my grief because my relationship to Norm was an uncommon one. I couldn't put into words how disappointed I was when the kidney I gave Norm failed him. It felt as if I failed him.

Upon returning from our honeymoon, Gary and Britton moved into our new home. Still actively grieving Norm's death, I tried to put on my happy face. Overnight, my life changed drastically.

I felt overwhelmed with my new roles, while battling enormous grief. In the midst of adjusting to a new husband, children, and the death of Norm, my Aunt Sandra's condition worsened. In mid-July, she lost her battle with cancer and one more time, my heart broke into pieces. I wondered if God had forgotten me. I'll be honest, negative tapes from my past cranked up and questioned my faith, or lack of it.

The idea that I had a death curse of some sort on me was beginning to look more likely, and although logic disagreed, my emotions weren't so sure. My spirit was so down and weary. All around me, there was death. I tried hard to look like I had it all together, but the truth was, I was just trying to keep myself from falling apart at the seams.

Never having been a mother before, I was at a disadvantage in my new role as a step-mother. I realized Bree and Britton were old enough that they didn't need mothering, but I also knew from personal experience, that we never out grow the need for our mother's love. There were many days I sensed in my spirit that Bree and Britton continued to actively grieve the loss of their mom and feared my presence was a constant reminder that she was not there. That is a horrible place to be, for them and for me. The next three months were tense at times as we all tried to live amongst each other as new family members. Bree, Britton and I were still strangers with heavy cloaks of grief on our shoulders. It wasn't quite so simple for all of us and we stumbled and tripped through that first summer together. God has a way of giving us grace even when we don't know to ask for it.

In August, Britton headed to Texas A&M for his first year of college. I sensed he was struggling with all of his life changes as well, but I didn't know how to connect with him. I suspected his heart was still grieving the loss of his mom, the move from his hometown and now, adjusting to his dad's new marriage.

One of the most helpful books I read during that time was *The Smart Stepfamily* by Ron Deal. Even with the healthiest people, blending families can be one of the most difficult things you'll ever tackle. Because Gary and my relationship had gone so smoothly, I automatically thought our family would blend just as easily. That was certainly an unrealistic expectation. Ron mentions in his book that blending families with adult children can take up to seven years before cohesiveness begins. After I read that, I was comforted to know we weren't that far off track.

When two unrelated families unite under one roof, it can resemble two powerful rivers merging with a magnanimous force. Stepfamilies definitely have their own set of issues, but they can also have their own unique bliss. One thing is certain, whether you're about to enter into a blended family or you're already in one, I lend you the following knowledge of what I learned walking down the blended family road.

1) Allow each family member adjustment time after you move in under one roof. Premarital counseling between the bride and groom won't prepare the family for the adjustments they're about to face. The adjustment period could easily last up to three years or more. Patience and compassion for one another will go far during this time period.

2) Strongly consider blended family counseling, both individually and as a family. This can be more useful after you have lived as a family unit for a few months. Only after living together are you able to identify the major differences in family traditions and expectations.

3) Implement a time when all members of the family are together, such as one night a week for family dinner. Set aside time for each member of the family to communicate how they feel they are adjusting to the new living situation. It's particularly important to communicate with one another in an open, non-threatening way.

4) Just as important, begin new family traditions within the first year. This could be anything from special ways to celebrate each other's birthday, to creating a new tradition at Christmas.

The important thing is to have everyone participate and create fun and enjoyable memories.

5)Last, but certainly not least, **pray together!** The magnitude of praying together is vast. Praying together fosters intimacy, trust and faith, which are extremely important for any family unit, yet aren't necessarily automatic with a blended family.

As a family, we've grown closer to each other over the years. The more we communicate, the closer we get. Time is a great resource in a blended family. Ask God for wisdom and patience as He shapes your new family to resemble the beautiful mosaic it will become.

****

Thanksgiving was around the corner and for the first time in my life, I was going to be the hostess for my family's huge Thanksgiving Dinner. Gary and I decided to have everyone come to our house to begin a new tradition. Both my sisters were able to be there that year. We could not remember the last time the three of us were together on a holiday since Dad's death.

Karen was grateful because she didn't want to have Thanksgiving at her house this being the first year without Norm. She, Kendra and Kyle desperately wanted a change of venue and knew it would be good for their hearts to be with all of us. All together, we hosted twenty-seven people and I was in holiday heaven. Every family brought a side dish and we had more food than we knew what to do with. As I heard the laughter at all the different tables, I silently thanked God for the gift He'd given me. I'd dreamed of hosting large family dinners. Finally, everyone came to our house and it was one of the best Thanksgiving holidays I'd ever experienced.

Our first Christmas as Mr. and Mrs. Gary Wells was wonderful, as well. The sense of belonging to someone was something for which I'd longed for many years and finally, I knew I was at the right place at the right time. Gary, Britton, Bree and I established a new tradition that year and it was such a great activity for us as a new family. We called it our Random Act of Kindness. We gave Britton, Bree, and ourselves, fifty dollars to randomly give away however we saw fit. Every year we come up with different ideas whether it be anonymously paying for a family's meal or leaving the fifty dollars at the register at Toys R' Us to apply to the next customer's bill. Our Random Act of Kindness was such great fun for us and the highlight of our Christmas holiday.

As my family expanded, we had several stops to make to visit people at Christmas and everything flowed well that year. Christmas Eve afternoon at JoMarie's with Papa Joe and Flo started off the holiday. We went to church with Karen and her family that evening, then we did a gift exchange with them and later returned home and exchanged gifts with Bree and Britton. Christmas morning we traveled to Dumas to be with Judy and Archie. I became more comfortable with their family as they were so kind to me. I did still struggle at times feeling a little out of place, but I did the best I could. God's grace got us all through some awkward times and I am so grateful for that.

That particular year, God brought five of my dear friends from my hometown back into my life. Four of us began Kindergarten together and all six of us graduated high school together. Through a series of emails, we finally agreed to meet for a weekend and thus began the rekindling of dear friendships. It never fails, we usually revert back to the silly girls we were in high school, but we don't care. Our stomachs hurt from so much laughter. There is tremendous comfort that comes from people who have known you all of your life and love you anyway. Our group, we fondly call, The SSG's (Same Sweet Girls), has continued to meet at least twice a year. Their friendship has been priceless to me and something I will cherish forever.

# Chapter
## Fifteen
*Forgiveness Wins the Victory*

In January 2007, I began a Writer's Life Group through our church and thus began the formal writing of the book you are holding in your hands. For many years, I journaled faithfully, but never wrote an actual book. Almost one year passed since the first whisper from God to write this book and I had not obeyed. *Who was I to write a book? Who would even read it anyway? What would people think if they knew all the unsavory details of my journey?* Thankfully, the discomfort of disobedience became insufferable and I knew I must overcome my fears and take action. After our first group meeting, I ambitiously thought I'd have the book finished by the end of the year with all the talented people as guides and encouragers. Of course, God had a much different plan than I.

It was a difficult struggle to begin the process of putting words on paper because as I remembered details about my childhood, a deep sadness enveloped me almost to the point of being paralyzed. Despite the fact that some healing had already occurred, many wounds were stuffed so deeply, I didn't even know they still existed. Decades separated me from those hurts and only God could escort me back to that place and I shuddered at the thought of returning.

Painfully, I wrote from my heart, revised, and wrote again. Through the course of many months of attending the Writer's Life Group, I only managed to complete the Introduction and first chapter! Thankfully, I had encouraging people in that group and I continued to write. As my heart relived some very painful memories, the tears flowed freely. There were many times I wondered if the only reason God whispered to me to write this book was so I could heal those deeply embedded wounds, especially if I couldn't get past Chapter One.

Despite growing in the Word, going through deliverances and maturing spiritually, the seven year old girl I was when Mom left me was *still* crying out for comfort. It wasn't until I began to write that she was ever allowed to completely surface. As I wrote about the night Mom left, I could vividly see the details as if it happened just minutes before, not twenty-five years in the past. I'd buried that memory so deeply, I was amazed at the pain that welled up inside me. In the midst of writing about that painful memory, two boxes were uncovered in my aunt's storage building. They'd been there for almost thirty years. When I opened them and rummaged through their contents, I couldn't believe the reaction I had. Years and years of letters I'd written Mom were in those boxes. Personal effects of hers I hadn't seen in almost three decades. Even letters Dad wrote her when they dated. Pain boiled up again and I could not control my weeping. *God, what is going on here? Why does this hurt so badly after so many years? What is wrong with me?*

The pain I endured from Mom leaving me was the deepest injury to my heart. God made sure I was held safe and secure in a tangible way by allowing Gary to comfort me while I wrote and tilled up wound after wound. I realize now that there was no possible way for me to dig that deeply into my childhood without

Gary's loving presence. I couldn't have done it and survived while I was single. Some days he'd come home from work and could readily see I'd been crying, yet without asking any questions, he held me tightly and allowed the tears to flow again. That is exactly how Jesus loves me. He allows me to come close and fall into His arms and He asks no questions. He comforts me until the hurt subsides.

My dear friend, Paula, also prayed over me many times asking God to heal the wounds that my writing opened. She completely understood what God was after from the beginning, which was to heal that core injury.

The pattern of digging, mourning, and healing continued as I typed memories onto my computer. I never knew what memory was going to cause an up rise in my emotions, but there were many along the way. The safety of a healthy marriage was truly my saving grace - a gift from God, indeed. Pastor Jimmy's words rang loudly in my heart, "We are meant to heal each other in marriage."

As I continued to forge ahead and write, I learned that forgiveness was imperative for me to live at complete peace. I carried unforgiveness around for so many years, the burden got heavier and more cumbersome. It began with my parents. When the two people I looked to for support, trust and love were completely unable to meet those needs, I buried my anger and resentment deep into my soul. No matter how far stuffed a feeling is, it will manifest itself in a behavior - usually in a destructive way.

For years, I didn't understand why I was hyper-critical of others, but I know now it came from that ugly root of unforgiveness. There are a multitude of negative results when lack of forgiveness takes up residency in our hearts.

My excuse list for not forgiving was endless, such as, "the person who hurt me never asked for my forgiveness," or "that person isn't truly sorry" or even, "that person needs to pay for what they did," (sometimes over and over). The slightest rationalization kept me from forgiving certain people.

Once I began to address my deepest wounds from childhood, I identified what unforgiveness had stolen from me for decades: love, joy and peace, just to name a few. I had far more to lose by not forgiving. That was a difficult concept to grasp, but once I did, I never let go of it.

When I wrapped my head around the idea of forgiveness, I was set free and determined to forgive all those I'd held in contempt, for perceived or real hurts. Even though my parents were deceased, I wrote them a letter expressing my feelings toward them and my subsequent forgiveness of them. The relief that came after I read that letter was amazing. It was as if I read it directly to them and I finally felt love and compassion for them in a way I'd never felt before.

Just as important as forgiveness is for us, it is equally important to seek forgiveness of those we've hurt. There were many people affected by my selfish, reckless behavior at different times in my life. I prayed for God to give me opportunities to seek their forgiveness, in person, if possible.

As I anxiously anticipated the opportune time to seek forgiveness of those I'd hurt, God prepared their hearts to receive my apology. Each time I asked forgiveness, I was delightfully surprised at their readiness to accept my apology and the immediate peace that overtook me. I never imagined I would get an emotional high from seeking someone's forgiveness. The freedom from that bondage gave me incredible joy.

The Lord answered a prayer I'd prayed since the first day of my transformation in 2003. Remember the night out at the bar, when my ex-husband's girlfriend and I exchanged some unpleasant words? (Okay, 'unpleasant' is a mild description.) As God changed my heart to reveal more of His desires, I prayed He would one day give me the opportunity to apologize to her in person. Four years later, that opportunity presented itself in the most unlikely place. A dear and mutual friend of ours was in the hospital after suffering a brain aneurism. As I approached the Critical Care elevator, the doors opened, and out she walked. Our eyes met briefly, and we murmured amiable "hellos." As she passed by me, I knew this was the opportunity I'd waited for.

"Can I talk to you?" I asked with hope in my voice. She turned and looked at me and, the words flowed out of my mouth, "I am so sorry for that night all those years ago. There is no excuse for my behavior; I just want you to know how sorry I am for all I said." With tears in my eyes, we embraced in a hug and she added, "Life is too short to hate someone that much." I couldn't have agreed with her more, as our dear friend lay helpless in the hospital.

Having that brief conversation removed a burden from my heart that had been there for years. Forgiveness is such a powerful thing. Its effects are life-changing and this was one of those instances in my life. There is not a price a person can put on the benefits of seeking someone's forgiveness. Again, I knew I was at the right place at the right time and God's hand was upon me.

I never want to be indebted to unforgiveness again. The dividends of forgiveness are much more lucrative. Consider what unforgiveness has cost you and ask yourself, "Can I continue to afford this?" My bet, the answer is no.

****

Writing this book facilitated my healing process and I was living my beautiful dream of being Gary's wife. Yet, there was one thing that still remained.

Since the day Gary and I married in May, 2006, I dreamed of having another wedding ceremony that was not heavy with grief and tears. My wedding day was one of the saddest days of my life and that's not how a bride wants to remember her big day. It was definitely not the wedding day of my dreams as I was barely able to stand on my weak knees. Though nothing could bring Norm back, I deeply desired to have a 'do-over.'

So, for four and a half years, I dreamed of a second wedding ceremony, complete with our friends and family, dry eyes and smiles, and of course, wedding cake. I didn't think that was too much to ask for after carrying around the heartbreaking memory of our actual wedding day for the past four years.

As our five year anniversary inched closer (May 2011) time healed much of my grief and I no longer desired a big wedding ceremony. Gary had worked long hours for several months and we hadn't been away together, on a non-work related trip in more than a year. (By the way, that's way too long.)

Although Gary was all for another ceremony to celebrate, I had something else in mind for our fifth anniversary and eagerly began to plan. I decided to have a vow renewal ceremony in Scottsdale, Arizona with just the two of us. My goal was to replace the sad memory I'd carried around for over four years with a new memory that brought a smile to my face. Since I wanted this to be a celebration of 'all things new' it was fitting to have a new wedding dress as well. (Okay, I couldn't get my original wedding dress zipped up.) I debated over the idea of getting a new wedding ring, but opted for a new center stone instead. I explained to Gary why I wanted 'all things new.' The memory I'd carried around of our wedding day was an important one, but not one that brought a smile to my heart. He completely understood. I told Gary all he needed to do was write new wedding vows and he obliged.

I called the resort prior to our arrival and arranged for reservations the night of our anniversary at their premier restaurant. For anniversaries, they provided a single-layer wedding cake. *Perfect!* I brought along a silver initial "W" for the cake topper.

Traditionally, most brides want something old, something new, something borrowed and something blue. The something old was a napkin from our original reception with our names and the date of our wedding, May 28, 2006. The something new was my beautiful wedding dress, which had me truly feeling like a blushing bride. The something borrowed was a single rose that was on our breakfast tray that morning in a vase. The something blue was a beautiful handkerchief my friend, Twilla, gave me with our names and our new vow renewal date embroidered in blue thread.

I carried my wedding dress on the plane, but Gary had no idea what was in my garment bag. That evening, he dressed in his suit and tie and went downstairs to wait on me to join him. Gary's job was to find a staff member of the hotel to take our picture. A few minutes later, I appeared at the top of a beautiful staircase, dressed as his blushing bride. Gary was at the bottom of the staircase and looked up when I emerged. His mouth dropped open and his eyes sparkled. He was so surprised to see me standing there in a wedding dress and veil. He summoned a staff member and they took pictures of us on that beautiful staircase.

With our new written vows in hand, we walked to a dimly lit courtyard that was perfect for our private vow renewal ceremony. As we read our new vows to one another, a new memory was in the making. I'd carried the grief of our wedding day for so long without recognizing its heaviness. The making of a new memory was just what I needed.

We proceeded to the restaurant where we enjoyed a candlelit dinner, a champagne toast and our wedding cake, which was also a surprise for Gary. The entire evening was absolutely beautiful and I couldn't have asked for a more perfect vow renewal day.

After we arrived home, I searched through the photos we took to create an announcement card. I thoroughly enjoyed putting the event together and sharing this with our family and friends. I made a new photo book of our vow renewal and replaced our framed wedding photo with a new one. Every time I looked at the photo from our original wedding, it touched a sad place in my heart about that day. Now, when I look at our wedding photo, I'm reminded that God heals our wounds and truly makes all things new.

Gary and I enjoyed our vow renewal weekend so much; we've decided to have one every fifth year. I love the idea of a new wedding dress and cake every five years! What a treat to look forward to.

**\*\*\*\***

Though the trials I've been through since my transformation have been tough, I realize there was no way I could have survived them as my old self. Thankfully, God has the most up-to-date GPS (God's Positioning System) and when I was terribly lost, God kept "Recalculating. . .Recalculating. . .Recalculating . . ." until I finally found the road that leads to life. I still get off course and God uses His GPS to recalculate my path, even now, no matter if I make a wrong turn, or completely miss the road altogether. He never tires of 'recalculating' for us, which is good news for this sometimes directionally challenged girl! Following Jesus doesn't mean we won't have struggles, but it does mean, we won't ever have to struggle alone.

Each trial I suffer through causes my faith to increase. Faith is not a bridge over all my troubled waters, but more like a life jacket to wear as I swim through them. I have great days and I still have bad days, too. But without a doubt, the great days far outnumber the bad.

Since I was such a 'late-blooming Christian' I eagerly soak up every knowledgeable word or teaching about God and His love for me. The concept of grace has been difficult for me to completely grasp. I am a constant work-in-progress. Sometimes, the most elementary teaching will give me the greatest revelation.

Andrew Womack writes in his book *Living in the Balance of Grace and Faith,* "Sin has already been dealt with by grace. God forgave your sins before you existed. Sin is actually a non-issue. People aren't going to go to hell for sexual immorality, murder, lying, or stealing. All those sins have been paid for. The sin that is going to send people to hell is the singular sin of rejecting Jesus as their personal Savior." *That* is the message of grace. It is not by anything I do that I am saved, but by God's free gift of grace through my faith in Jesus. He only asks us to believe.

For some, like me, that is good news. For others, that message may still be hard to grasp because it seems too simple. All I can testify to is what I've lived through myself. I know who I was before I surrendered everything to Jesus on February 23, 2003 and I know who I am today. The difference is undeniable, if only to myself. I learned the most from being broken and humbled. For years, I covered my brokenness and ran from it, not believing even God could put me back together. But one night, while at the wrong place at the right time and after a dose of humility, I allowed God to take that brokenness and shape me into the person I was always meant to be. It seems inconceivable that something that caused such anguish in my life would be the very thing that brings me joy today. Only a *Redeemer* could accomplish a feat such as that in any of us. When God heals, the shame vanishes and the victory is truly ours!

I encourage you to look inside yourself for the wounds that are weighing on your heart and dragging you down. You may not even know how deep they go, but one thing is certain; when you gently peel the layers back, healing finally begins. It doesn't happen instantly and it does take a great deal of work, but the rewards of living with freedom, joy and peace are beyond anything you can dream or imagine.

My hope is that you will allow God to take the broken pieces of your life, love you right where you are and mold you into the beautiful child of God you were always meant to be.

Go ahead. He's waiting for you with open arms.

## References

Chapter 7: *Conquering Codependency: A Christ-Centered 12-Step Process* by Pat Springle (www.mcgeepublishing.com)

Chapter 8: *Boundaries: When To Say Yes, When To Say No, To Take Control of Your Life* by Henry Cloud and John Townsend

*Why Good Things Happen to Good People* by Dr. Stephen Post, Phd & Jill Neimark

Chapter 10: *Our Secret Paradise*: Jimmy Evans (www. marriagetoday.com)

*Facing Shame: Families in Recovery* by Merle Fossum and Marilyn Mason

Chapter 14: *The Smart Stepfamily* by Ron Deal

Chapter 15: *Living in the Balance of Grace and Faith* by Andrew Womack

# About the Author

Photo by Twilla Woolsey

Dawn Wells and her husband, Gary, reside in Amarillo, Texas with their "Two Dogs," Shorty and Lovey. (Gary's dachshund, Schnitzel, resides in Dumas, Texas with Jatawn's parents, Judy and Archie.) Dawn and Gary are anxiously awaiting their first grandchild by their daughter, Bree and son-in-law, Daniel, who also reside in Amarillo. Britton, their son, lives in Fort Worth, Texas where he has begun his professional career in commercial real estate appraisal.

Dawn is a first-time author who has come miles away from the little girl who grew up in Sunray, Texas. She no longer fears "swinging the bat, or shooting the ball." She is active in several different hobbies and ventures as her entrepreneurial mind continues to dream of one day owning her own business with her husband. She also desires to minister with her sisters one day as well. Not every swing is a hit, but she doesn't care. She's learned the valuable lesson that if you never swing the bat, you'll never hit the ball-ever!

Dawn enjoys photography of nature, animals and especially horses. Her insatiable love for horses began after attending a women's retreat in Lubbock, Texas (www.soulpurposeexperience. com) where she fell in love with the mystique of horses and their intuitive natures. She volunteers at Horseplay at Mesquite Ranch in Amarillo to help cure that insatiable need to be in the presence of horses. (www.horseplayatmesquiteranch.com)

Dawn is active in her community serving the downtrodden, the poor and the broken-hearted. She has a true compassion for the less fortunate. She also enjoys leading women to the hope of Christ through her testimony of faith. She speaks for women's groups, fundraising events and facilitates Bible studies to share the gospel with all. She deeply desires to leave a legacy of faithfulness.

www.dawntaylorwells.com

Dawn and Gary - Vow Renewal May 28, 2011

Terri, Tanya and Dawn

Norm's Family and Dawn/Christmas Card 2004

Papa Joe's 94th birthday with Gary's entire family-August
2011

Back left to right:  Daniel, Britton & Gary
Front:  Dawn & Bree - Christmas 2011

Shorty and Lovey

Robin, Melissa and Dawn, Chicago 2010

Pam, Cindy, Tammy, Dawn & Paula - GNO "Girls Night Out"

SSG's (Same Sweet Girls from Sunray)
Back L to R: Mary, Amy, Treon
Front L to R: Misty, Dawn, Dean

CPSIA information can be obtained at www.ICGtesting.com
Printed in the USA
LVOW061324120113

315463LV00005B/10/P